The Bilingual Revolution Series

TBR Books

A Program of The Center for the Advancement of Languages, Education, and Communities (CALEC)

Our Books in English

The Gift of Languages: Paradigm Shift in U.S. Foreign Language Education by Fabrice Jaumont and Kathleen Stein-Smith

Two Centuries of French Education in New York: The Role of Schools in Cultural Diplomacy by Jane Flatau Ross

The Clarks of Willsborough Point: The Long Trek North by Darcey Hale

The Bilingual Revolution: The Future of Education is in Two Languages by Fabrice Jaumont

Our Books in Translation

Die bilinguale Revolution: Die Zukunft der Bildung liegt in zwei Sprachen by Fabrice Jaumont

La revolución bilingüe: El futuro de la educación está en dos idiomas by Fabrice Jaumont

ДВУЯЗЫЧНАЯ РЕВОЛЮЦИЯ: БУДУЩЕЕ ОБРАЗОВАНИЯ НА ДВУХ ЯЗЫКАХ by Фабрис Жомон

La Révolution bilingue: Le futur de l'éducation s'écrit en deux langues by Fabrice Jaumont

Upcoming

چومون فابريس بلغتين يُكتب التعليم مستقبل اللغة ثنائية الثورة

双语革命 双语革命：两种语言铸就教育的未来 by Fabrice Jaumont

Rewolucja Dwujęzyczna : Przyszłość edukacji jest w dwóch językach by Fabrice Jaumont

バイリンガル革命の日本語訳出版の支援をお願いします by ファブリース＝ジュモン氏は、

La Rivoluzione Bilingue by Fabrice Jaumont

By the Same Authors

Kathleen Stein-Smith. *The U.S. Foreign Language Deficit: Strategies for Maintaining a Competitive Edge in a Globalized World* (Palgrave-MacMillan, 2016).

Kathleen Stein-Smith. *The U.S. Foreign Language Deficit and How It Can Be Effectively Addressed in the Globalized World: A Bibliographic Essay* (Edwin Mellen Press, 2013).

Kathleen Stein-Smith. *The U.S. Foreign Language Deficit and Our Economic and National Security: A Bibliographic Essay on the U.S. Language Paradox.* (Edwin Mellen Press, 2013).

Fabrice Jaumont. *Partenaires inégaux: fondations américaines et universités en Afrique* (Editions Maison des Sciences de l'Homme, 2018).

Fabrice Jaumont. *Stanley Kubrick: The Odysseys* (Books We Live by, 2018).

Fabrice Jaumont. *The Bilingual Revolution: The Future of Education is in Two Languages* (TBR Books, 2017).

Fabrice Jaumont. *Unequal Partners: American Foundations and Higher Education Development in Africa* (Palgrave-MacMillan, 2016).

THE GIFT OF LANGUAGES

Paradigm Shift in U.S. Foreign Language Education

Fabrice Jaumont & Kathleen Stein-Smith

\

TBR Books
New York

TBR Books is a program of the Center for the Advancement of Languages, Education, and Communities. We publish researchers and practitioners who seek to engage diverse communities on topics related to education, languages, cultural history, and social initiatives.

TBR Books
146 Norman Avenue
Brooklyn, New York
www.tbr-books.org | contact@tbr-books.org
Front Cover Illustration © Jonas Cuénin

ISBN 978-1-947626-22-5 (paperback)
ISBN 978-1-947626-23-2 (eBook)
Library of Congress Control Number: 2018914029

Contents

11

12

"We are at a critical point in our nation in which we can continue to hold on to our monolingual past or embrace a multilingual and more inclusive future. The Gift of Languages helps us prepare and understand the necessary paradigm shift to adopt and implement a multilingual curriculum and mindset in our schools and communities. Co-authored by two pioneers and experienced experts in the bi- and multilingual education space, the book is a must read for educators, policy makers, community leaders, students, and interested parents who want to make meaningful changes now."
– Andrew H. Clark, Ph.D. Chair, Dept. of Modern Languages & Literatures, Fordham University

"The Gift of Languages should awaken all Americans, especially the policy makers, for the need to raise future generations of multilingual citizens to compete and thrive in our global community. One of our founding fathers and presidents, Thomas Jefferson, spoke to and acted upon the need for teaching languages when he founded the University of Virginia; as a nation, we have not lived up to his words and actions. Let us remind ourselves that we started out a linguistically and culturally diverse group of peoples that came together to build a strong nation over the years. Linguistic diversity is the gift that our nation needs to give itself!"
– Francesco L. Fratto, President, The Foreign Language Association of Chairpersons and Supervisors

"Mastering languages is essential for communicating with and understanding others, respecting each other, and appreciating our heritages and our roots. The Gift of Languages offers an invaluable toolbox for policy makers, educators, families and students who are already working in the field of language and those who hope to create the kind of paradigm shift that the authors advocate. The book provides cogent arguments in favor of expanded language learning at all levels, and especially argues in favor of expanding the breadth and variety of multilingual educational opportunities already

spreading in public school systems from Utah to Louisiana to New York and beyond. The authors cite examples of the "Bilingual Revolution" already underway and provide the kinds of arguments and examples that resonate for educators and drive policy towards furthering the way we value language education in the United States. The book is indispensable for anyone interested in the future of foreign language education."
– Jane F. Ross, Ph.D. President and Founder, French Heritage Language Program

Over 60% of people on the planet are bilingual or multilingual — which suggests that this is the norm for human beings — and multiple studies demonstrate the cognitive, social, political, and financial benefits of bilingualism. Yet in the United States, we regularly hear news stories about people being shamed, bullied, and sometimes violently harmed for speaking other languages, even when they also speak English.

Accessibly written, this book offers detailed arguments for both *why* and *how* the nation should embrace and promote linguistic diversity. Options for adults are expertly addressed, yet the authors invest even greater passion and detail in promoting early educational programs in which no child is left monolingual. I can think of no better way to shift our nation's view of itself from "English Only" to "English Plus" and create a more inclusive society.

We need a roadmap, and this book clearly lays out the territory and possible trajectories as it motivates us to make the journey.

Kimberly J. Potowski, Ph.D.

Professor in the Department of Hispanic and Italian Studies
University of Illinois at Chicago

The emergence of newer international standards and the focus on STEM education are transforming entire educational sectors. Yet, as schools focus more attention on developing global competencies and 21st century skills in their pedagogy, it has become critical to re-engage educators and school communities with the goals of language education, multilingualism, and multiliteracy while promoting interconnectedness, empathy, and mutual comprehension among our youth. With this in mind, it is important to understand the potential of multilingual education as it can serve our societies' new expectations and provide the right tools for success to our younger generations.

This book explores the many advantages of multilingual education and sets the stage for a new paradigm in our approach to teaching and learning languages. It touches on the issue of the foreign language deficit in the United States and the changes that need to occur in our schools to better serve our children and our linguistic communities. The book also explores the growth of dual-language education in recent years and the connection between both multilingual programming and solving the United States' foreign language problem.

The discussion on language education in the United States has never been neutral. Moreover, business and geopolitical priorities have traditionally provided substantive direction and exerted significant authority over U.S. educational language policy. Yet, this debate needs to move towards viewing multilingual education as an essential approach for our society, and as something that should be prevalent among educational policymakers.

In our opinion, it is time to change the paradigm of foreign language education to meet the urgent needs of our students, and of equipping all of them with the strong language skills they need to navigate - both socially and professionally - an increasingly open and competitive world.

To change the paradigm is to create school environments where languages are more present, taught in class and lived outside the classroom, in a common project led by school communities and in which the practice of languages will combine pleasure and efficiency.

To change the paradigm is to create a shared language culture in schools first, by mobilizing the skills of teachers from all disciplines and by encouraging all actors to share the gift of languages.

To change the paradigm means unleashing energies and encouraging the creativity of all actors in linguistic communities, valuing their ideas and practices, and developing strategies for successful language learning and teaching.

To change the paradigm is to invent an American way of working that reconciles our linguistic heritage with the political choice of multilingualism for our future.

This involves adopting a more collective approach to teacher support, mentoring, and the sharing of good practices. This also involves providing information, coaching, and tools to multilingual families seeking to create language programs in their schools or sustain their linguistic heritage. It is our hope that this book's readership will include educators, language teachers, school leaders, school boards, program directors, scholars, policy makers, and parents who want to join forces in building the future of education and investing in the multilingual capital of our nation.

Fabrice Jaumont and Kathleen Stein-Smith
New York, New York
October 15, 2018

THE GIFT OF LANGUAGES

Chapter 1

Why a Paradigm Shift is Needed

In considering languages in contact in the globalized and interconnected world, it is important to reflect upon the significance of language in the development of a global worldview and of global citizenship values, and to decide whether a multilingual world, or a world with a single global *lingua franca* is preferable. From that initial reflection and decision stem multiple choices for individuals, for organizations and institutions, and for the government that impact educational, social, and cultural practices. It all depends on the future envisioned.

In order to bring about a paradigm shift in the prevailing lack of interest in foreign language learning in the United States and in order to lessen language-based or language-related inequality, effective foreign language advocacy, based on a collaborative partnership including educators, business, government, and parents, is necessary.

If the decision is made for multilingualism, planning must seek buy-in from community language stakeholders, including parents, in order to ensure a sustainable education program. The next step is considering which organizational structures need to be developed to support the program. Families and individuals have made personal decisions as to whether to maintain and support their heritage languages, and/or to learn additional languages. Communities have decided whether or not to develop and implement bilingual or dual-language immersion programs, or even whether to offer one or more foreign languages as part of the curriculum. If a decision is made to encourage the learning of additional languages, it is important to consider the supply of qualified teachers, appropriate books, and other materials needed to implement and to sustain the initiative. It may also be necessary to consider funding options, including external funding, to support any necessary teacher training and curriculum development.

Every paradigm shift is accompanied by difficulties that must be overcome before it can be reproduced on a large scale. At the heart of these difficulties are funding and school budgets. Access to school materials in the target language is a problem frequently encountered by educators. The scarcity and cost of materials are significant obstacles, especially for schools that do not have sufficient resources. Overcoming these obstacles requires strong collaboration between school administrators and foundations and associations that can make critical contributions to these streams. The success of many bilingual chapters depends on the continued support of these successful partnerships.

A challenge that is equally important is the difficulty of recruiting multilingual teachers. The laws that regulate the conditions for teaching in a public school in the United States vary from state to state. Thus, the pool of candidates is significantly reduced. National rather than state certification could be a way to combat these administrative difficulties. In addition, only a small number of teachers have American citizenship or a green card, and while schools may grant different visas, these remain temporary. Some states allow this process of granting visas *only if* no other certified American teacher can do the same job. This significantly reduces opportunities for schools seeking to hire native speakers of the target language to create a more immersive environment. This problem is even more prevalent in remote schools than in large urban centers. Luckily, there is a solution that could work in the long run: students currently enrolled in a bilingual stream, completing their education and becoming teachers themselves, have the potential to become certified, qualified, and competent bilingual educators.

While individuals and groups often think of their language as part of their personal and cultural identity, and linguists think of languages as a means of communication, and in terms of their history, structure, and relationships to other languages, it is also necessary to think of languages and linguistic skills in terms of their role as assets to individuals, workers, employers, nations, and international organizations.

Languages open doors and provide opportunities, and language skills empower in terms of geographic mobility, ability to communicate, access to information and education, and ability to interact effectively on the world stage. In a globalized and interconnected world, it is also necessary to think of languages in terms of influence and of soft power, "the ability to encourage collaboration and build networks and relationships" (Gray, 2017). It has also been said that foreign language learning increases tolerance (Thompson, 2016; World Economic Forum, 2017).

Multilingualism as the Norm

Many Americans view monolingualism -- specifically, speaking only English, as the longstanding status quo. However, this may not necessarily be the case. Not only do people around the world often speak more than one language, but they have done so throughout history. In fact, it is estimated that between 40% and 50% of the world's population speak more than one language -- many speak multiple languages. Many consider English the global *lingua franca*, but the reality is that only 25% of the world's population speaks English.

However, relatively few Americans speak a language other than English, with estimates ranging between 10% and 25%, largely including recent immigrants to the United States and their children and family members. In addition, a minority of Americans study a foreign language –fewer than 20% of K-12 students in the United States study a foreign language (American Councils, 2017), and only 7.5% of college and university students are enrolled in a course in a language other than English (MLA, 2018). With over 60 million

Americans speaking a language other than English in the home (Ryan, 2013), but relatively few Americans speaking or studying a language, there is a clear US language paradox -- a resolutely monolingual nation that is, and always has been, a nation of immigrants.

While, historically, there have always been many languages within the United States, these languages disappeared largely from schools and organizations during the 20th century, and immigrant languages have been typically largely lost by the third generation. Most non-English speaking children arriving in the United States lose their original language by the second generation. Grandparents and grandchildren can no longer communicate with each other. Sometimes even parents and children cannot communicate properly.

These parents were convinced of the many multigenerational benefits of preserving their respective legacies, laden with the treasures of literature, culture and history, and maintaining a sense of pride and identity. All understand that a bilingual stream contributes to a dynamic, rich and diverse society. More than anything, they understand that multilingualism is a family story, a story of preserving identity. It is a story so powerful that it goes beyond language learning itself. In today's society, English has the power to annihilate other languages, languages of great value, that transmit rich cultures, stories and knowledge. With this dominant linguistic power come the forces of Americanization and assimilation, which are often brought to extremes where children discover for themselves the enormous weight of English in our monolingual environment. As a result, their mother tongue often appears to them in a negative light.

To prevent students from giving in to this pressure, we must teach students, in addition to their parents, schools, and communities, that being bilingual is the best thing. Although language learning is a global concern, this paradigm shift begins locally, in neighborhoods, schools and communities. Multilingualism is of great value to all of us. The more we will be able to communicate with members of our community, as well as those of others, the stronger the fabric of our society will be. If school authorities develop clearer guidelines and support mechanisms, initiatives of this kind will be able to operate more effectively, maximizing their chances of success. The hardships, stamina and perseverance described here show that our entire education system needs to be remodeled. Schools must finally be able to respond to the growing demand for language education by embracing the idea of multilingualism.

In an increasingly globalized and interconnected world, monolingual Americans may be at a disadvantage in a multilingual world, personally, professionally, and as global citizens. Furthermore, our society may be less divided than it would otherwise be if we had more understanding of other languages and of our own multilingual heritage.

In the context of the United States, English-speaking monolingualism is a real obstacle to the development of society, which misses out on the enormous linguistic resource that its citizens represent. As the world learns English and becomes multilingual, the United States is lagging behind. It is imperative that in this country we are able to read, write and communicate in more than one language. If we do not manage to abandon this sense of self-sufficiency, it is our children who will suffer by not taking advantage of the personal, social, professional and academic benefits that multilingualism could offer them.

Knowing several languages and cultures can give Americans these advantages. Cohorts of high school and university students should land in the world of work, ready to face the global market. Multilingual education has the potential to foster respect and tolerance, while understanding cultures different from ours is crucial today. When parents demand this type of education, a paradigm shift is in motion. Language education continues to show incredible results, but its development is slowed by a lack of national mobilization around multilingualism. We need a paradigm shift to establish the prevalence of multilingual education in this country and elsewhere for the benefit of all.

Over the last fifteen years, language communities in many cities in the United States have initiated and developed dozens of bilingual streams in several languages, some of which have transformed schools and the education of our children. In particular cases, it has transformed language education models into a viable and desired solution for all families, bringing many benefits to our school communities that are in the United States or elsewhere in the world. These programs are more than just language courses. They allow children to better understand the cultures that surround them by offering them intercultural exchanges within the school. The programs strengthen and support our linguistic heritage and promote the value of cultural and linguistic diversity in all societies of the 21st century. When one thinks of the globalized world in which we live today, it is no longer possible to cling to the idea that only one language can suffice.

Once multilingualism becomes the rule and no longer the exception, qualified candidates will be less difficult to find. By giving them time to grow, bilingual streams will become sustainable courses. More and more reassuring signs are showing that Americans now want to expand their horizons, look beyond the confines of their own country and recognize the richness and diversity of their current culture. It is becoming increasingly common for Americans to speak a language other than English at home, in part because of immigration. To speak more than one language fluently is gradually becoming the norm, especially in big cities. In addition, parents' interest in multilingualism is increasing as they discover what early language education can offer their children. The cognitive, academic, social, personal and professional benefits are undeniable. Multilingualism and multiliteracy are now seen as assets, not only for their cultural virtues but also for their ability to produce "citizens of the world". There is no doubt that multilingual education should be accessible to every child in the United States and the world.

In our increasingly interconnected, miniaturized and fragile era, schools around the world are striving to give young people the skills, abilities and sensitivities that will enable them to become autonomous, engaged and productive citizens. Language teaching and learning and the so-called "bilingual advantage" are resurfacing in schools, large and small, all over the United States. It has become clearer that parents and teachers are looking for an ideal of teaching or learning in two languages.

America's Language Deficit

The US foreign language deficit is a paradox that has become even more apparent if US foreign language skills are compared with those of Europeans, who routinely study one or more foreign languages beginning at relatively earlier grade levels. In addition, more than half of working adults in the EU report the ability to converse in one additional language, with many able to hold a conversation in two or more additional languages.

While these European language skills are impressive on their own, they are even more so when considered within the context of the EU core value of multilingualism, operationalized in the school system by an educational objective of *plurilingualism*, or "mother tongue + two."

This US foreign language deficit has been the subject of research reports, Congressional Hearings, national security initiatives, and -- most importantly -- has been part of the public conversation for decades, the current public conversation beginning with the publication of the report of the President's Commission, *Strength through Wisdom*, in 1979, followed by *The Tongue-Tied American*, by Senator Paul Simon, in 1980.

Interest in foreign language skills increased briefly as International/Global Studies became a popular college major, and interest in international/global education increased in response to globalization. However, the percentage of Americans studying other languages, especially at the college and university level, has continued to decrease.

Foreign language educators, supported by foreign language stakeholders in international education, in business and in government, have not idly stood by -- far from it. Among the numerous research reports and conferences on the US foreign language deficit, the 2003 NAFSA report, *Securing America's Future: Global Education for a Global Age*, the critical languages initiative, the 2006 CED report, *Educational and Global Leadership: The Importance of International Studies and Foreign Language*, the 2007 report, *International Education and Foreign Languages: Keys to Securing America's Future*, the 2009 Language Flagship report, *What Business Needs*, the 2013 conference *Languages for All*, and the most recent 2017 reports -- AMACAD's *America's Languages*, the New American Economy's *Not Lost in Translation*, and the American Council's K-12 foreign language enrollment survey have made the case for foreign languages abundantly clear.

However, it is the 2007 MLA report, *Foreign Languages and Higher Education: New Structures for a Changed World*, that has provided a road map for K-16 educators, for foreign language advocates and supporters across the disciplines, and for foreign language stakeholders in business, government, and in our communities. This clearly written, relatively brief report is noteworthy both in the strength of its ideas and in its clarity of language, accessible to even the non-specialist. Within the context of a globalized world, the report defines translingual and transcultural competence as the goals of foreign language learning, and goes on to call for interdisciplinary collaborations, pre-professional curricula, and K-16 partnerships.

However, as the 10th anniversary of the MLA report was observed in 2017, the consensus was that its impact was limited -- far more educators were aware of the report and of its call to action than were actually implementing the goals outlined in the report within their institutions.

In addition to *Foreign Languages and Higher Education*, the MLA has published its Enrollment Survey since 1960, during which time foreign language enrollment has decreased from 16% to 7.5% of college and university students in the US, with the most recent report confirming that the decrease is part of an ongoing trend.

Foreign language learning in the US stands at a crossroads. In fact, our "widespread hostility to seriously learning foreign languages has become legendary" (Stearns, 8). If we do not effectively address the US foreign language deficit, our young people risk being marginalized and even left behind in a globalized, interconnected multilingual world.

In order to effectively address the US foreign language deficit, it is necessary for us to draw inspiration from our past and present in order to develop a sustainable framework for foreign language learning in the US. A strategic partnership of foreign language educators, along with foreign language stakeholders and supporters in business, government, and in our communities -- especially in our communities -- is essential.

While the overarching goal of building the foreign language skills we need is shared, foreign language learning is the quintessential example of a global reach in need of a local touch. Foreign language is the ultimate global competency, but the reasons for learning another language are unique to the individual and to the community, and the community context and available resources vary locally.

Looking to the present and to the near future, the campaign for foreign languages must be guided by the shared goal of accessibility of foreign language learning for all interested learners. A successful campaign will be guided by the best in theory and practice in change management, innovation, strategic social and cause marketing, lobbying, and even blue ocean strategy and design thinking. However, it is also a grassroots campaign with specific local goals and objectives -- there is an opportunity for all foreign language advocates and supporters to play a role.

However, it is also important to look to our past to understand the enduring importance of parents, families, and communities in education in general and in foreign language learning in particular. It is often said and written that "it takes a village" to raise our children, and languages, part of our personal cultural identity, are very much a part of the fabric of our family, our friends and neighbors, and our communities in general. At this turning point in foreign language learning in the US, it is more important than ever to reach out to parents and communities and to value and respect their engagement in our cause.

While the government and education departments in every state have traditionally negatively viewed the use of languages other than English for the education of young Americans, middle-class families are today engaged in this paradigm. The shift begins at the base, by parents who recognize the value of multilingualism as part of their American identity. This is precisely what makes this paradigm shift so good: it reminds us that multilingual education is an American tradition, although it is surrounded by tensions, controversies and challenges, as we show later.

This paradigm shift finds the hope of a tradition of multilingual education that reminds us that all Americans (of different ethnic identities, social classes and countries of origin) have multiple linguistic and cultural practices. In this paradigm shift, American parents whose linguistic heritage of children is imbued with Arabic, Chinese, English, French, Japanese, Italian, German, Polish, Russian and Spanish words, understand the importance of these practices. According to them, a multilingual education is not only a way to reconnect with the past, but to recognize a multi-lingual American present and to forge the possibilities for a more inclusive future for all children.

In addition to the role of language and languages in the globalized world, our own communities are increasingly multilingual, and increasing opportunities for our children to learn our own languages and those of others will foster understanding and harmony in our own US society. The time to act is now.

A shift in conventional thinking
about foreign languages

Ideally, we would learn additional languages in a way that closely resembles mother tongue acquisition, through experiential learning complemented by classroom learning, from early childhood. Unfortunately, that is often not how we learn additional, or second, languages, which are often learned later in life and in a classroom setting that does not offer the opportunity to develop authentic language skills through authentic communicative and cultural experiences.

The good news is that classroom learning now offers the opportunity for learners to develop second language skills using authentic texts and media, either in person or through online resources. Learners can develop foreign language skills through comprehensible input, where use of authentic language empowers learners to comprehend even above their specific language skills level, through Teaching Proficiency through Reading and Storytelling (TPRS), which engages the innate love of storytelling to develop language skills, immersion, and a more traditional foreign language education.

In addition, the proliferation of online media, including television, films, news, etc., allows language learners and enthusiasts to access target language content freely online, through subscription services like Netflix, now known for its quantity of foreign language content, and through language learning apps like Duolingo.

Once the decision is made to learn a language, the learner needs to decide whether classes or self-directed learning are the better fit, and whether texts or online and media materials are more appropriate. It is also important to note that these choices and decisions are not mutually exclusive. A learner in class is always free to ameliorate the class experience with additional in-person and online language learning. Similarly, the independent self-directed learner has countless online resources available, including apps, but can always decide at any point to take a class, purchase a textbook, or borrow books from a library. Employers who value foreign language skills for business reasons have the possibility of funding foreign language study, either through tuition reimbursement, or by offering classes on site.

The decision of whether or not to learn a language, when to begin language study, and how to learn a language are, of course, largely personal. Many college students lament their lack of foreign language skills when a study abroad, or international volunteer or professional opportunity comes up. However, on the other hand, students face the time management challenge of college and university courses, jobs, and other commitments. For many, college and university may not be the time to begin or continue language study, and that raises the question of the importance of an early start, which could ensure that -- by the time students are at the university level -- they would have already acquired proficiency in one or more languages, and be ready to engage in experiential learning and volunteer experiences that could empower them professionally and as global citizens.

Returning to the question of learning a language through course work, or as an independent self-directed learner needs, the question of cost often arises, as courses and textbooks may be a financial challenge for many students, and the time/opportunity cost of language study versus other courses and opportunities may tilt away from foreign language study at the college and university level. Again, the importance of an early start to continued foreign language study–whether in a traditional or immersive program–in order to reach proficiency before the onset of adult obligations, is even more clearly highlighted.

If, indeed, a student opts for a foreign language course, there are in-person, online, and hybrid/blended choices, at different price points, with community colleges often providing the best economic value. There is also the possibility of studying through a commercial language school, which typically emphasizes communicative, instrumental skills, or the possibility of a traditional or short-term study abroad, which may emphasize cultural learning.

One of the challenges faced by any foreign language learner is finding the time, whether it involves finding the time to do required course work and to study for midterms or finals, or whether the independent self-directed learner needs to allocate time for foreign language study in an already-busy schedule. The important thing to remember is that even a brief amount of time -- if set aside for language learning on a regular basis -- can be sufficient for progress to be made. The most important commitment the learner can make is consistency.

If the learner chooses the path of independent self-directed learning, it is important to develop a personal learning plan including goals, materials, and time lines. A foreign language educator, librarian, or knowledgeable language enthusiast can help in charting the individual's self-directed learning plan. Factors to consider in creating this plan include the financial budget, the time available for foreign language learning activities, and the learner's preferences, but a balanced program could be based on a textbook, media, and apps, along with individualized cultural learning experiences based on individual interests. Online badges and certificates, along with a local community, as well as external socio-cultural resources such as the Alliance Française, Societa Dante Alighieri, etc., are just a few of the options available.

Language learning is more readily available than ever before due to the proliferation of online authentic cultural and language material, but more difficult than ever before, due to the intense pressure of the globalized workplace. However, the good news is that even with a modest financial budget and limited time, anyone can learn another language.

The most important factor is the will and motivation to learn one or more additional languages. To cultivate this motivation, we need to increase awareness among students and those already in the workforce of the advantages of foreign language skills and cultural knowledge in both personal and professional life, and in our lives as global citizens.

It is interesting to remember that one of the most popular reasons given by Americans for not studying or learning another language is that there is no need to since English is the global *lingua franca*. However, the worldwide web of information, education, and entertainment is remarkably multilingual, and monolingual Americans will only have easy access to a small part of this global web of information, education, entertainment, and communication.

One of the primary uses of language is to obtain information, and the internet/web is often the first place that people look for information on virtually any topic: personal, professional, or educational.

However, not all information is readily available, or even available at all, in English. While English is the most frequently used language on the internet, accounting for about 30% of internet content, all 6 of the UN official languages are in the top 10 most frequently used languages on the internet. Each one of us experiences the internet, and its seemingly limitless content, generally in terms of the languages we know.

But those who know only English may miss out on almost three-quarters of the internet. On the other hand, if you happen to be a speaker of a language spoken by few, but widely scattered people, the internet is a wonderful means of creating a sense of community for users of that language.

It is also important to consider books published in terms of language use. The United States leads in terms of revenue, followed by China, Germany, the UK, and France, but China leads in terms of titles published, followed by the United States, UK, France, and Germany. As far as newspapers are concerned, India leads the world, and print readership continues to grow.

Many Americans believe that the best in education is to be found solely in US universities where the medium of instruction is English. However, while American, British, and Canadian universities are to be found among the world's top universities, there are also many universities in the global top 100 in China, Japan, South Korea, France, Germany, and more. There are many equally wonderful educational opportunities for those who speak additional languages.

Another use of language is to seek out entertainment in the form of film, literature, and broadcast media. In terms of feature films, although feature films are produced in many countries, the overwhelming majority are produced in the top 5 film-producing nations, with India in the lead, followed by the United States, China, Japan, and France.

There are nearly 3B social media users globally, with Instagram with the most followers worldwide and with Facebook having the highest number of monthly users worldwide. In terms of active users worldwide, Facebook leads, followed by YouTube, WhatsApp, Facebook Messenger, WeChat, and Instagram. Yet again, monolingual Americans may miss out on countless opportunities to join the global conversation.

International organizations have specific language policies and official languages depending on their mission and membership. Even though an official language of an international organization may be English, meetings, members, issues, and initiatives can be worldwide, and the monolingual American might often be out of the loop on important mission-related and social conversations.

As always, in order to develop the needed paradigm shift in conventional thinking about foreign languages -- and, in particular, about the unique role and special place of Spanish and French in American history and society -- it is essential to use the best theory and best practices of change management, science of persuasion, and social marketing to make the case for Spanish and French as quintessentially American languages, and of blue ocean strategy to make the case to audiences and communities who may never have envisioned learning additional languages as part of our history and heritage, as well as part of the professional and global skills set of the 21st century. If Americans are to have full access to information online and in print, to education, to entertainment, to social media, and to global engagement, multilingualism is an essential global competency.

Even though English is present around the world, three quarters of the world's population does not speak English, and much of the world's mission- and work-related communication, as well as social communication, takes place in other languages, making it more essential than ever for US students to have the opportunity to study one or more additional languages. If Americans are to play a role in effectively addressing global issues, we must speak the languages of others and have an appreciation of their cultures. An equitable system would provide this opportunity, with access for all, through our public schools.

Chapter 2

The Case for Foreign Language Skills

A n asset can be defined as "an item of value" or "something useful," and foreign language skills fall easily into both categories (Merriam-Webster). Foreign language skills are a personal and cultural asset to individuals in terms of the ability to better enjoy travel, literature, and those they come in contact with either during travel or in their local communities. Simply put, they make life so much more interesting, in so many different ways. An estimated half of the world's population is bilingual (Grosjean, 2010).

Foreign language skills are a resume differentiator (Vanides, 2016), an asset to workers, and have been associated with higher earnings and improved employability. All things being equal, an employee with foreign language skills is less likely to be laid off than a monolingual co-worker.

Foreign language skills are an asset to businesses and employers, ranging from the smallest businesses with multilingual clients and customers to the largest multinational firms. These businesses may actively recruit new employees with foreign language skills and cultural knowledge, maintain a record of the foreign language skills of employees for use as needed, or develop a language strategy or policy.

Multilingualism is an asset to communities at all levels, including nations of the world, many of whom have one or more official languages. Canada, Switzerland, Belgium, and Luxembourg are just a few of the many examples. In 2017, Montreal was named the best city in the world for students, and one of the reasons given was the opportunity to earn a university degree in two global languages, French or English. Globalization has caused more contact among languages than ever before, with New York City home to 800 languages (Lubin, 2017), and London home to more than 300 (BBC, 2014).

New York's Bilingual Revolution includes dual-language immersion programs in a dozen languages in the NYC public schools, along with numerous heritage language programs. Both NYC and San Francisco have recently hosted Dual-language education Fairs.

Multilingualism is a core value and asset of many international organizations, including the United Nations (UN), the European Union (EU), and the International Olympic Committee (IOC). The European Union and the United Nations have opted for multilingualism, specific nations and organizations have adopted one or more official languages, and multinational corporations have at times adopted a language strategy (Neeley & Kaplan, 2014).

In July 2017, in his comments on the biennial report on multilingualism, UN Secretary-General Guterres affirmed that, "I care deeply about multilingualism, a core value of the United Nations."

The EU has embraced multilingualism as a core value and has encouraged multilingualism, often referred to as "mother tongue + 2" in schools and through its Erasmus program of study abroad for university students. In the EU, over half (54%) of adults report the ability to speak an additional language, 25% speak two additional languages, and 10% speak more than two additional languages (Eurobarometer, 2012).

Often the question becomes which language(s) to learn, and the answer is both simple and complex -- it really depends on personal and professional reasons, with the personal motivation, geographic location, and professional needs all considered in the final decision. One factor, however, that is often overlooked is the role of related languages -- that is, if one learns a Romance, Germanic, Slavic language, for example, additional languages within that same family may be more easily acquired.

Supply and Demand

The importance of foreign language skills in the United States workplace is increasing, and demand for bilingual workers has more than doubled in the last 5 years. The top six industries for multilingual employees are healthcare, hospitality and customer service, finance, law enforcement, education, and social services (New American Economy, 2017).

International business, import/export, and foreign investment also add to the significance of foreign language skills in the workplace. In any business or organization, it is always best to speak the language of the customer, consumer, or client. As in the quote attributed to Willy Brandt, "If I'm selling to you, I speak your language. If I'm buying, *dann müssen Sie Deutsch sprechen!*"

Approximately 11 million US jobs depend on exports, and some of those jobs require, or are enhanced by foreign language skills (International Trade Administration, 2017). In 2017, the top export destinations for US products and services were Canada, Mexico, China, Japan, and the United Kingdom, making French, Spanish, Chinese, and Japanese languages of potential importance (US Census, 2018).

Foreign-owned companies employ seven million US workers and contribute $900 billion to the United States GDP, with New Jersey, South Carolina, and New Hampshire having the largest percentage of the workforce employed by foreign-owned companies (Bialik, 2017).

Tourism accounts for more than 10% of the global GDP ($7.6 trillion), with employment at 292 million, 1 in 10 jobs globally (WTTC, 2017), many of which require or are enhanced by foreign language skills. In addition, in the $45 billion global language services sector, three of the top five language services firms in the world are headquartered in the United States, creating demand for translators, interpreters, and localization specialists. In the U.S., 50,000 people work as translators and interpreters (Gala-Global, 2018), and demand for translators and interpreters in the United States is predicted to increase by 18%, or "much faster than average," from 2016-2026 (*Occupational Outlook Handbook*, 2018).

Over one million international students attend US universities, the top countries of origin being China, India, South Korea, Saudi Arabia, and Canada, making Chinese, Indian languages, Korean, Arabic, and French useful in providing student services and making new students feel welcome. Over 300,000 US students study abroad, with the UK, Italy, Spain, France, and Germany being the top destinations, making Italian, Spanish, French, and German part of preparation for study abroad (Institute of International Education, 2017). The economic impact of international students is estimated at 36.9 billion contributed, and over 450,000 jobs supported (NAFSA, n.d.). Yet there is a widespread shortage of foreign language teachers in the United States (US DOE, 2017).

Also, in contrast, the supply of US workers with the needed foreign language skills is lagging, and US workers are not generally taking steps to acquire foreign language proficiency. Moreover, the perceived value of foreign language skills in the workplace has also been demonstrated in the United Kingdom, where only 34% of employers are satisfied with the level of foreign language skills, and French, German, and Spanish are highest in demand (CBI, 2017).

Economic Asset

According to the World Economic Forum, "language is an essential component of competitiveness" (Chan, 2016). Foreign language skills are an economic asset both to the individual in their career and to nations in their economic growth and security. Individuals may pursue careers where foreign language skills are required, or careers where foreign languages are an advantage. Importantly, additional skills include critical thinking, active listening, and even creativity–skills that are often part of the foreign language learning experience.

In a survey of graduate international business students on competitive advantage resulting from foreign language skills and cultural knowledge, the results were 82% and 89% respectively (Grosse, 2004). An earlier study found that economic and employment factors played a major role in foreign language choice (Grosse, 1998).

The global language industry is estimated at $40 billion, with a projected growth rate of 6.5-7.5% annually and more than 300,000 working as translators or interpreters worldwide. In the United States, there are more than 3,000 language services firms, and more than 50,000 are employed as translators and interpreters in the United States. Three of the top 5 language service providers in the world are located in the United States (Gala-Global, 2018).

Job opportunities for translators and interpreters are predicted to increase by 18% (much faster than average) between 2016 and 2026, and job opportunities for foreign language teachers at the postsecondary level are predicted to increase by 10 - 14% (faster than average) (*Occupational Outlook Handbook*, 2018).

It is noteworthy that the six official languages of the UN are often found at the top of language rankings. Bloomberg developed a ranking of the most useful languages for international business, with English, Mandarin Chinese, and French as the top three (English, 2011). The World Economic Forum has developed a Power Language Index ranking, with -- again -- English, Mandarin Chinese, and French the top three, and the top six include all six of the UN official languages -- Arabic, Chinese, English, French, Russian, and Spanish (in alphabetical order).

In his discussion of the 2017 report, *Not Lost in Translation: The Growing Demand for Foreign Language Skills in the Workplace*, Mc Munn (2017) affirms that the demand for bilingual and multilingual employees continues to rise in the U.S. and U.S. businesses lose nearly two billion dollars a year because of a lack of language skills and cultural knowledge.

An earlier report, (Language Flagship, 2009), examines the significance of language skills in developing new a business and keeping it, and the risks of over-reliance on translators, interpreters, and contractors in compensating for the lack of language and cultural skills within the organization. Describing the need for interpreters and translators in the United States, (Kurtz, 2013) confirms the growing need for language service professionals in the military, law enforcement, government, and the corporate sector.

In a discussion of skills ranked as most important for Google, a Google study (Meaghan, 2018) confirmed that people skills -- including communication and listening, ability to understand different perspectives, empathy toward others, critical thinking skills, and the ability to make connections -- are among the most important. It is interesting to note that these are routinely learned in the foreign language classroom. In a description of the benefits of multilingualism in the workplace, Kokemuller (2018) includes better pay and more job flexibility for those with language skills.

Although language skills tend to be associated with greater earnings, supply and demand can impact the benefit of a specific languages. For instance, Poppick (2014) cites research confirming the demand for the German language in the workplace.

However, the value of foreign languages skills in business is not a new concept, with Cornick & Roberts-Gassler (1991) recommending that accounting and business majors study a foreign language in order to be prepared for international business and greater employment opportunities. Conner (2014) confirms that US monolingualism negatively impacts US economic growth, due to missed opportunities in the global marketplace, even as the UK takes steps to increase foreign language skills among the workforce.

Perspectives from beyond the United States

However, a paradigm shift in attitude toward foreign language learning is needed beyond the United States and beyond the anglophone world. According to the all-party parliamentary group on modern languages, the UK loses about £50 billion a year in contracts lost due to lack of foreign language skills (Jolin, 2014).

A research study on the benefits and costs of the European Multilingual Strategy (EMS) found that foreign language learning, "Mother Tongue + 2," enhances mobility and inclusion (European Parliament, 2016).

Grin, Sfreddo, & Vaillancourt (2010) have examined multilingualism in the workplace from an economic perspective, finding that in both a society and workplace impacted by globalization, language skills broaden access to more rewarding careers.

In a study of the benefits of multilingualism in Quebec (Vaillancourt & Lemay, 2007), research demonstrated the benefits of multilingualism for both anglophones and francophones, as well as impressive growth in ownership of the Quebec economy by francophone firms since the passage of the Official Languages Act in

1969. A recent review of the literature on the economic benefits of multilingualism in Canada confirms that multilingualism has brought not only historical, but also economic and social benefits, and that multilingualism is part of Canada's value proposition, enhancing individual, organizational, regional, and national success and competitiveness (Canadian Heritage/Patrimoine canadien, 2016).

Among the workforce skills that contribute to foreign investment, Euronews includes language skills as a factor in the decision-making process. In her discussion of the reasons why multilinguals make the best employees, Hogan-Brun (2017) outlines that the cognitive skills that bilinguals have are also valuable workplace attributes, going further to describe the impact of diversity on creative problem-solving.

In a discussion of the findings of the British Academy's Born Global project, Murray (2014) describes the impact of the global economy on the need to develop a workforce with international and language skills, highlighting the need for greater practical and professional language skills.

In a study of how linguistic and cultural barriers impact business (Economist Intelligence Unit, 2012), it was found that while companies are now more aware of the importance of doing business internationally and, as a result, realize the importance of language skills and cultural knowledge in effecting cross-border collaborations, many organizations are recruiting employees with these language skills, but that more remains to be done. In a study comparing export performance of Swedish, French, and German SMEs, Bel Habib (2011) found a relationship between export success and use of a variety of market languages.

The ELAN study (2007) found that 11% of export SMEs were losing business due to lack of language skills and established a clear linkage between language skills and success in the export sector. In a study of language skills in the enterprise sector in Ireland, (Forfás, 2005) research examined the impact of foreign language skills on foreign investment and employment in the foreign-owned sector and mentioned the potential loss of international opportunities to domestic firms lacking foreign language skills.

In his research study on the value of foreign language learning, Schroedler (2018) examines the relationship between Ireland's lack of foreign language skills, the presence of many multinational corporations (MNCs) in Ireland, and the country's active pursuit of foreign investment. In describing the importance of languages as a career asset, Hazelhurst (2010) confirms that Germany and France/Belgium are among the most important trading partners of the UK, making German and French invaluable in the workplace.

In a study of the returns on foreign language skills in Turkey, Di Paolo & Tansel (2014) examine foreign language skills as human capital and the extent to which they are rewarded in the employment marketplace, finding differences among languages, professions, and the level of linguistic skill. Williams (2011) examined language use in the workplace in several European countries and found varying rates of return corresponding to the extent of tourism in the particular country. The only exception was the UK, where earnings appeared unaffected by the use of additional languages in the workplace.

In conclusion, it is not surprising that the Indian government has actively promoted making Hindi one of the official languages of the UN and is reported to be prepared to spend "up to four billion rupees ($63 million)" to achieve this goal. Beyond economic value, foreign language skills are closely linked to their role in influence and "soft power."

The Business of Language

In the United States, foreign language skills and cultural knowledge offer a pathway to many careers, in education, government, business, cultural institutions, and international relations. In addition, foreign language skills have been generally associated with increased income.

It is of critical importance that we develop and maintain equitable access to foreign language education and to the development of bilingual skills. If children are not able to learn bilingual skills in our public schools, many will be unable to take advantage of these opportunities for financial reasons, potentially creating "haves" and "have-nots" in terms of language learning, multilingualism, and cultural knowledge.

The size of the language services sector and the language learning sector only serve to confirm the value placed on language skills worldwide. The language services sector is valued at $45 billion globally, employs over 55,000 people in the United States alone, and three of the top five language service companies in the world are located in the United States. Localization and translation are among the fastest-growing industries in the United States, and the language industry is one of the best sectors in which to start a new business. In addition, employment for translators and interpreters in the United States is predicted to increase by 18%, 2016-2026, much faster than average. Foreign language skills and cultural knowledge are also part of global talent, with a recent survey of employers revealing that 41% give preference to multilingual applicants.

The language learning sector is also considerable, with Rosetta Stone generating $185 billion in revenue in 2017, and Berlitz estimated revenue at $468 million for the same period. Duolingo's valuation is estimated at $700 million, and overall online language learning revenue is estimated at $4 billion.

The Commodification of Language Learning

If our public schools do not provide and support language learning and bilingual skills, parents and learners who want multilingualism for their communities will need to seek alternatives. However, whether the learner attends traditional or online classes through a for-profit language school, or whether they learn through an online program or app, the important thing to remember is that there are usually financial costs involved, which is not the case if these essential skills are offered through public schools.

It has been estimated that, for an English-speaker to learn Chinese, the highest language in both time and financial cost, the cost would be £66,035 ($87,220). In addition, the global online language learning market is predicted to grow by 19%, 2017-2021, and online companies like Rosetta Stone compete with apps like Duolingo, as well as against organizations like Berlitz. In addition to being part of our educational system, language learning is big business worldwide.

It is also important to bear in mind that many for-profit language schools do not stress the cultural knowledge associated with the language, but rather purely linguistic and communicative skills. In this case, even if the learner has the financial means to purchase language instruction, that language education is unlikely to include the cultural component that is routinely part of public school and college foreign language learning.

There would actually exist a double inequity, depriving those unable to pay to acquire a personally and professionally valuable skill and the associated benefits. In addition, even those who could afford language instruction through a for-profit organization risk being deprived the cultural knowledge associated with the target language that can make it more rewarding, both personally and professionally.

Both the facts of increased salary and employability for those who have foreign language skills and the costs that can be incurred by individuals if they are forced to learn one or more additional languages through the for-profit sector demonstrate the need and value of having language education as part of the school curriculum from the start.

Languages, Influence, and Soft Power

It is possible to travel the world and to see visible signs of American culture and its language, English, almost everywhere. However, it is more difficult to determine whether seeing an American movie on a cinema marquee, hearing an American song, or seeing a local young person wearing a T-shirt or baseball cap of a US professional sports team indicates actual understanding or appreciation of US culture. Recently, French President Emmanuel Macron's use of the English language on several public occasions has brought both praise and criticism.

Language is far more than a set of grammatical rules and multiple vocabulary lists, it is part of our personal and cultural identity, and just as individuals compete in the global marketplace, nations and their languages compete in terms of prestige and influence.

People around the world make decisions -- whether to invest the time, effort, and money to learn another language, and if so, which language to learn, and how. At the present time, English and French have the largest number of learners worldwide. In comparing languages in terms of influence, Bloomberg found that English, Mandarin Chinese, and French are the most useful languages for international business. Similarly, the World Economic Forum found that the same 3 languages, in the same order, are the most powerful in the world, making an additional connection to the fact that the most powerful languages were those languages which were also official languages of the United Nations.

The UN and government-sponsored entities also work to promote specific languages. For example, the UN promotes the study of its six official languages, just as the Alliance Française, Societa Dante Alighieri, Instituto Cervantes, Goethe Institut, Istituto Camoens, and the British Council seek to promote French, Italian, Spanish, German, Portuguese, and English respectively. Several US government programs actively promote the English language, most notably the State Department Bureau of Educational and Cultural Affairs, whose subtitle reads "promoting mutual understanding."

English First actually ranks countries and regions by English language skills with the Netherlands, Sweden, and Denmark being the top three, and Panama, Singapore, and Saudi Arabia with the most significant improvement. In addition, global clusters of innovation are associated with cultural flexibility and language skills. However, the importance of soft power resides in the fact that people from all over the world are interested in another culture and its language, and may even wish to study there, work there, or relocate there.

At the present time, France is the world leader in soft power, wielding influence worldwide well beyond its geographic borders and the size of its population, as other languages have done in the past -- think Latin, Spanish, etc.

However, it is important to consider the factors involved in acquiring and maintaining soft power and influence. While language learners may not necessarily be adherents of the target culture's current politics and social issues, an engagement with, and even an affection for, the target culture's history, culture, values, etc. may be an important part of the process -- for example, the influence of French and Italian culture and language beyond their geographic borders. It is interesting to note that the *Organisation Internationale de la Francophonie* website cites both the French language and shared humanist values as organizational cornerstones.

That is a challenge for all of the cultures and the nation states, as well as for their languages that may seek an international role and global prominence. While partisans of a certain culture and its language may not necessarily support all the vagaries of international politics and relations, the values of the target culture, as expressed in its literature, art, media, and social values and lifestyle -- as well as in its approach to sometimes difficult contemporary issues -- are, nonetheless, important in building and sustaining global support and buy-in from many diverse cultures.

Therefore, in addition to proactively supporting culture and language learning beyond national borders, it is important for nations desirous of expanding their cultural, linguistic, and general influence beyond their borders to be mindful of how their nation -- and its language and culture -- appears to potential admirers both near and far away.

Whether locally or globally, actual influence -- the ability to bring people to see things from your perspective -- is far subtler and more complex than it may seem at first glance. English is often described as a global *lingua franca*, and is in fact an influential and powerful language, but other languages remain desirable and useful, in terms of the appeal of the target culture and its influence.

Nation states desirous of building, expanding, and maintaining their influence and soft powers need to frame their campaigns, not only on the psychology of influence and power of persuasion, but on maximizing all that is best in their cultural heritage and values, in order to win over a new generation.

Multilingualism as a Public Good

In addition to its role as human capital, multilingualism is a public good that can foster not only good will among various segments of society, but also global engagement and global citizenship. As such, foreign language education falls within the scope of public-school curriculum just as other subjects deemed to be related to the public good are. The global worldwide language learning industry, with English the most popular language to study worldwide, offers a glimpse at what the situation could be for Americans who, realizing the need for language skills, would have to purchase them at considerable financial cost.

Chapter 3

The Societal Benefits of Multilingualism

L anguage skills and cultural knowledge provide personal benefits, including cognitive, cultural and professional advantages. Multilingualism also plays a significant role in global citizenship. In addition, diversity -- including linguistic diversity -- benefits organizations, communities, cities, and even countries. The United Nations supports multilingualism as beneficial to the global community, and it is a core value of the European Union.

It also plays a significant role in innovation, and many of the world's most successful countries, regions, and cities are linguistically diverse, and while this impact has been intensified by globalization, examples of the power of linguistic diversity can be found throughout history.

The Relationship of Diversity, Creativity, and Innovation

Places known for innovation are also places that attract creativity and innovation from all directions, bringing together different ways of seeing and doing things, fostering the nonlinear divergent thinking characteristic of creativity. The result of these community and workplace interactions across languages and cultures is a synergy that enhances the creativity of the group.

Just as teamwork builds on the presence of more than one person's perspective to solve a problem, a diverse team may develop solutions based not only on the perspective of more than one person, but on the perspectives of team members who may see the world -- and the problem at hand -- differently through the lens of a different language and culture.

Multilingual Switzerland ranks first in the 2017-2018 Global Competitiveness Index, followed by the United States. The rest of the top 10 includes Singapore, Netherlands, Germany, Hong Kong SAR, Sweden, United Kingdom, Japan, and Finland. It would be easy to assume that the multilingualism of Switzerland and Singapore may not be related to their global competitiveness, but the true significance of multilingualism lies beneath the surface.

In the United States, for example, more than 60 million speak a language other than English in the home. Sweden, Singapore, Germany, and Finland are in the top 10 of the English First Proficiency Rankings. In the UK, more than 4 million speak a language other than English in the home. Both Chinese and English are official languages of both Hong Kong and Singapore. Japan may be the only outlier in terms of multilingualism and global competitiveness. In terms of the most innovative economies, again Switzerland and the United States lead the list, followed by Israel, Finland, Germany, Netherlands, Sweden, Japan, Singapore, and Denmark. While it is interesting to note that many of the same countries appear on the list, newcomers Israel and Denmark have a high degree of linguistic skill. The top 7 global cities are London, New York, Paris, Hong Kong, Tokyo, Singapore, and Seoul, the only outliers in terms of multilingualism are Tokyo and Seoul.

While diverse teams and their divergent thinking are critical to global competitiveness and innovation, a challenge is to maximize the advantages of this diversity while minimizing its potential disadvantages through building an environment of trust and acceptance of differing viewpoints.

Developing the Global Skills Set

Just as innovation and creativity are needed more than ever before to effectively address complex global issues, globalization and increased global mobility have made it relatively easier to bring together diverse perspectives in any neighborhood communities large and small, but especially in the global cities that are financial and social magnets for people from around the world.

While it is impossible to predict and ensure creativity and innovation, it is very possible to develop the kinds of communities and organizations where the interactions of diverse thinkers may result in the synergistic effect that drives innovation and creativity. It is possible to foster the development of language skills and cultural knowledge by encouraging everyone–children in school, and workers in the workplace–to develop the ability to look at problems through different perspectives, or different cultural and linguistic lenses. In doing so, we can encourage divergent and nonlinear thinking and facilitate conversation among people from different backgrounds, with different worldviews, who may bring the additional element needed to forge a better solution and pathway forward.

If, indeed, we want our children to have every chance to be more adept at examining issues and problems, not only critically, but from multiple perspectives, the place to begin is in our local public schools, where foreign language education is needed from the earliest levels. In a learning environment that mirrors our increasingly diverse society, it is possible to expand our children's horizons as we prepare them to better address the challenges of the present and of the future.

Global mobility is on the rise. Creative professionals and international students are choosing those communities and organizations that are most attractive to them and where they will thrive, maximizing their potential.

In order for our communities and cities to be the world's best and brightest and to offer the best future for our families and local communities, it is necessary to focus on globalizing our towns and cities, beginning at the earliest age to inculcate the values and skills set of the global citizen and the global professional in our children through our public schools.

This means educating our children about other languages and cultures and empowering them through multilingualism to maximize their potential in a globalized world and workplace.

It also means working together, beyond the classroom, to strengthen the commitment of our communities to develop an atmosphere of hospitality, trust, and understanding, and beyond that, to develop the social and cultural environment and lifestyle that will not only appeal to globally mobile talent, but also to our own children, the heart of our global city, now and in the future.

People have always learned other languages, and often, the natural course of events is for them to learn while living in an area where their mother tongue is not the predominant local language. In a sense, they are "immersed" in the target language, hearing it and seeing it all around them.

Immersion education is an adaptation of this natural course of language learning to the school or classroom and is generally considered the method most likely to lead to a successful learning outcome. There has even been research that has demonstrated that the brain activity of immersion learners most closely mirrors that of the target language mother tongue speaker.

Immersion language learning exists in many countries around the world, and is sometimes referred to as multilingual education, or dual-language education, the latter term the more frequently used in the United States. In the United States, as of 2011, there were 448 immersion programs, with the largest number in the state of Utah.

Spanish, French, and Mandarin Chinese are the most frequent languages of instruction, accounting for 42%, 22%, and 13% of programs respectively.

Immersion programs vary, and there are different types of immersion programs. Programs vary as to the age at which children start the program, the amount of instructional time spent in each language, and the number of grades through which immersion is available. Programs can also be considered as offering total immersion, partial immersion, and two-way, dual-language immersion. They also can be described as early, middle, or late immersion depending on the age/grade at which immersion begins.

Reasons for implementing immersion programs include the need for bilingual skills in both the globalized workplace and in our multilingual society. As immersion learners tend to have better academic outcomes, immersion programs can be a means of fostering academic achievement. In addition, shared language and cultural skills can bring a community, a city, or a nation together.

Selected Examples of Immersion Programs

Well-known programs in the United States include the Concordia Language Villages and Middlebury College. The Concordia Language Villages, a program of Concordia College, have existed since 1961 and provide youth, adult, and family language immersion experiences. Middlebury College, known for immersion for over 100 years, also offers summer programs for high school students.

There are immersion programs available privately and through public schools. However, public school programs are accessible to all. The following selected examples offer some perspective on the range of programs available in US public schools. In New York City, for example, there are about 180 programs offered in nine languages (now, 12). In Utah, and in Portland, Oregon, about 10% of elementary school students are in dual-language programs, and

North Carolina and Delaware are among the states seeking to increase the number of such programs. Numerous Dual-Language Immersion (DLI) programs exist in Georgia public schools, including the middle and high school levels, through Georgia's DLI Initiative, offering programs in Spanish, French, Chinese, German, and Japanese. In Louisiana, CODOFIL, the Council for the Development of French in Louisiana, has 26 immersion schools in eight parishes, and more than 100,000 students are studying French.

Utah has the third largest number of DLI programs in the United States, with about 140 schools benefiting 34,000 students in 2017. Strange as it may seem, DLI programs in Utah, a state geographically isolated from the main economic centers, are growing despite a population that is not very diverse ethnically and linguistically. Foreign language immersion was designed, supported and implemented through the vision of political figures who identified the state's language needs and their potential for business, administration and education. In 2008, the Utah Senate adopted the International Education Initiative, providing funding to schools to open bilingual streams in Chinese, French and Spanish. German and Portuguese were added later, and Arabic and Russian are planned for the coming years.

Utah's multilingual initiative follows a partial immersion model where students receive half of their education in the target language and the other half in English. Each class has two teachers, one who teaches only in the target language in the first half of the day, and another who teaches English the rest of the day. Most courses start in Kindergarten, which number very few. Once in high school, most young people enroll in advanced language courses and take the AP World Languages and Cultures exams in the third year. During the high school years, they can take, through a hybrid learning system, university-level courses offered by six leading universities in Utah. High school students are also encouraged to learn a third language. This set of pathways represents an important step in the evolution of language education in the United States.

Fairfax County, Virginia, offers both world language (one-way) immersion and dual-language immersion in the primary grades. The Princeton, NJ, public schools offer a Spanish-language DLI 50-50 model program Kindergarten through Grade 5. Minnetonka offers an example of high school immersion, offering the Seal of Biliteracy and the International Baccalaureate, in addition to AP and Beyond and immersion elective options.

A recent report on the Portland Public Schools showed that DLI students out-performed non-immersion peers in reading test scores and that English language learners reached English language proficiency in greater numbers. The benefits listed by the Georgia DLI Initiative, part of the World Languages and Global/Workforce Initiatives, include second language and cognitive skills, better performance on standardized tests, intercultural competence, longer-term benefits in the workplace, and higher attendance rates and lower drop-out rates than students in regular programs.

Challenges to Immersion Programs

Challenges include implementation of new programs, program design and structure, curriculum, materials, and shortage of qualified teachers. Immersion programs may also not have the necessary resources. In addition, students may have varying levels of proficiency in both L1 and L2. Terminology and assessment vary from state to state, making it more difficult to make comparisons and to determine which policies and practices are most effective.

A shortage of qualified immersion teachers exists, partially due to the decline in foreign language majors in recent decades and partially due to the increasing popularity of immersion programs that reach out internationally for teachers. While this can help, lack of a consistent local supply of qualified teachers makes it more difficult to establish a sustainable immersion program. In addition, more teacher training programs specifically intended for immersion teachers are needed.

As far as second language skills are concerned, they tend to increase more slowly in the more advanced grades, with students more likely to use English rather than the immersion language, and the English speakers do not tend to progress beyond the intermediate level in their second language.

The lack of programs beyond the primary grades is caused in part by the shortage of appropriate teachers at the high school level also able to teach in a second language and the lack of high school subject curriculum and materials in the target language. The lack of these resources makes it challenging to develop business proficiency and pre-professional skills in the target language.   More K-16 collaborations are needed to ensure maximization of multilingualism in the workplace through interdisciplinary career pathways.

Immersion Works

Immersion programs are increasing in popularity because they work. Not only do benefits include better second language skills, but they also include cultural skills. Importantly, these linguistic and cultural skills offer workplace advantages in addition to personal, cognitive, and social benefits.

They also offer opportunity, especially through our public-school programs, as immersion students tend to achieve better academic outcomes overall. Benefits include increasing bilingual skills among English language speakers, as well as opportunities for speakers of other languages to improve their English language skills. For this reason, equitable access to immersion programs is essential.

While immersion is increasing in popularity, reflected in the development of new and expanded programs, it is important to focus on the development of sustainable immersion programs through expansion of teacher training, development of K-12 curriculum and materials, and learning from best practices.

Most importantly, the emphasis on cultural skills and cultural knowledge along with language may foster a more harmonious society and better opportunities for all.

Chapter 4

Bridging the Language Gap in the
United States

Relatively few Americans speak a second language, and among those who do, it is primarily a language learned and spoken in the home. Yet, there are several major issues for language educators and advocates here, including support of heritage language learners and their skills, encouraging English speakers to begin continued foreign language study to proficiency, and developing English language skills among non-English speakers.

Nearly 11 million K-12 public school students are enrolled in a foreign language, and nearly one and a half million college and university students are enrolled in a course in a language other than English (American Council, 2017; MLA, 2018). Foreign language learning may occur in a classroom, online, or in a hybrid, or blended, setting. Classroom-based learning may either be in an immersion or traditional setting.

While large numbers in the United States speak another language and significant numbers of students are enrolled in foreign language learning, there is ample room for expanding foreign language learning if even a small percentage of those claiming one or more ancestry groups were interested in learning their heritage language. Access and time/opportunity/financial costs are barriers to language learning.

In addition to the importance of language as part of our personal cultural identity, as part of our communities, and as a career asset, language skills play a role in our ability to interact with others in a globalized world. Without language skills, Americans are often at a relative disadvantage when working in a transnational team or group, where other participants are likely to be able to understand and speak multiple languages.

Even as students, the decision whether or not to study abroad is often limited by a student's lack of language skills. While over one million international students from around the world study in the United States, only 300,000 US students study abroad, and over 10% of that number – 39,000, study in the UK, where English is spoken.

Language Is What Makes Us Human

Language is generally considered the defining characteristic of humans, enabling us not only to communicate, but also to record our experiences and to learn from our own past and from the experiences of others. There is even a gene specific to language, found only in humans. While there are many reasons for learning other languages, it is this one defining characteristic of language that not only separates us from other species, but also from each other, as language expresses and defines what we see and how we see it.

The benefits of foreign language skills, and of multilingualism and multiliteracy, are often expressed in terms of personal and professional benefits, and as cultural, cognitive, and social advantages, all of these reflect the role of language as part of the human experience and of human life. It is this shared human experience that makes it all the more important to learn the languages of others.

Language is both a communicative and creative tool. Language is essential to communication, whether in a brief social conversation, a formal debate, or through news media, literature, and the arts. As such, it enables us to understand and appreciate the ideas of others, and to learn from the past. It is a creative tool in that it allows us to work alone or with others to create or develop ideas. It also allows for creative expression in literature and the arts.

Although we share common languages, each person's use of language is unique, and different languages may emphasize a different part of any given concept or experience. And that is exactly why we should learn other languages – in order to better understand the words and worldviews of others, without relying entirely on translation and interpretation.

Reading literature in the original language provides exposure to authentic language, with access to the exact words chosen by the author often providing insights into culture, whereas any translation involves an intermediary, the translator, and the translator's interpretation of the author's meaning.

Access to great literature in the original language is one of the wonderful benefits of learning one or more additional languages, but similar benefits come to us from non-fiction, and from spoken language in film, theater, and other media, when we can hear the original authentic text or script without any intermediary, possibly capturing nuances that would otherwise be lost in translation.

Knowledge of the local language is a definite advantage in doing business abroad. While official meetings may be conducted in English, or in the official language of the company, the social interactions that surround any business meeting are likely to take place in the local language, with the person who speaks only English missing out. The English-speaker misses out not only on the purely social aspects of the interaction, but also on the opportunity to build those personal relationships that are often even more important to business success outside the United States. It is also important to bear in mind that, for those who live in other countries for business reasons–while they may be able to get by with English in the workplace even while missing out on some of the business and social nuances–living in an area where you do not speak the local language can be difficult at best.

It is important to remember that even when we are reassured that everyone speaks English, that may actually be a fallacious assumption. One of the most frequently given reasons for why Americans do not speak other languages is that they believe that the world speaks English. While English may be widely spoken and studied, it is not the most widely spoken language in the world, but rather third, after Mandarin Chinese and Spanish. In fact, according to the British Council (2013), 75% of the world population does not speak English.

However, it is also important to remember that -- when in a country or region where English is not the official or predominant language -- showing respect for the local language and culture by speaking some of the local language and by demonstrating some knowledge of the local culture is an important step in communicating on a level playing field with local business partners, neighbors, and friends.

The balance of power among languages has changed throughout history, from the Latin of the *Pax Romana*, to Global English, but the key take-away is that the story of language, and of languages, is all about the people who speak them and their role in the world of their era.

For those of us in the United States, it is critical to remember that -- in business -- it is essential to speak the language of the customer or buyer. Most importantly, we must remember that although English is only the third most widely spoken language in the world, and only one quarter of the world population speaks English, only one in four Americans feels that they are capable of holding a conversation in a language other than English, and fewer than 20% of K-12 public school students study a foreign language.

The disconnect is too large to ignore between the importance of foreign languages in the world, and in our own US–where two-thirds of Americans claim at least one foreign ancestry, where millions speak a language other than English in the home, but also where the number of Americans who speak one or more additional languages and the number of students who study a foreign language is minimal.

Chapter 5

Bringing about a Paradigm Shift

I n order to bring about a paradigm shift in attitudes toward foreign languages and in the status of foreign language education in the United States, any initiative for foreign languages needs to be grounded in and framed by theory and best practices in change management, social marketing, cause marketing, the psychology of influence, disruptive innovation, the elements of successful grassroots political campaigns, and blue ocean strategy. The elements of the campaign for foreign languages can help effectively address the United States foreign language deficit by providing an integrative approach, embracing all foreign language stakeholders with many complementary goals, but one dream of building foreign language skills in the United States.

Change Management

According to John Kotter, effective change management begins with "a sense of urgency," which in the case of foreign language learning in the United States, is clearly warranted. The remaining steps in the 8-step process also include – building a coalition of support; developing a vision, and associated strategies and tactics; attracting volunteers; taking action; generating short-term wins; sustaining momentum; and incorporating change into the organizational structure. In terms of planning a campaign for foreign languages, there is much to be learned about building buy-in and, especially, in creating "a sense of urgency," from change management theory.

Social Marketing

Social marketing–not to be confused with social media and social media marketing, although social marketing may use social media as a method–has the goal of influencing behavior for the public good. As a campaign for social good, the campaign also needs to be based on the theory and best practices of social marketing, which adapts the strategies and tactics of marketing and uses them for the greater social good. In Kotler and Lee's *Social Marketing: Changing Behaviors for Good*, the strategic social marketing planning process is outlined in 10 steps – the social issue and focus; SWOT situational analysis; target audiences; behavior objectives and target goals; target barriers, the competition, and influential others; a positioning statement; marketing mix strategies (the 4 Ps – product, price, place, and promotion); monitoring and evaluation; budget; and planning for implementation and sustaining behaviors. From social marketing, it is essential to bear in mind the importance of getting the message to target groups and communities who are the most likely to benefit from foreign language learning, but who may face the highest opportunity and opportunity cost barriers.

Cause Marketing

An extension of corporate social responsibility (CSR), cause marketing involves corporate partnerships, and issues involved with clearly identifying objectives, choosing a cause partner, and developing the partnership (Rosica). Although the campaign for foreign languages is a volunteer undertaking, there are always costs, and cause marketing offers a path to raising needed financial support, through the always important corporate social responsibility (CSR) of many private sector enterprises. The identification of appropriate and suitable corporate partners and the development of a sustainable partner relationship are of the highest priority.

The Psychology of Influence
and the Science of Persuasion

Persuasion is at the heart of a successful campaign, and any campaign needs to be grounded in the psychology of influence and the science of persuasion. Robert Cialdini has identified six principles of persuasion – reciprocity; scarcity; authority; consistency; liking; and consensus. In the message of the campaign, whether in-person or via online and social media, it is important to incorporate the elements of the psychology of influence and the science of persuasion and it is especially important to establish a positive relationship with prospective groups of language learners through common ground and similarities of goals and aspirations.

Disruptive Innovation
A Grassroots Political Campaign

Disruptive innovation, a process described by Clayton Christensen, describes a bottom-up approach, which could pertain to an early start to foreign language education that would produce very proficient students at the high school level, in turn disrupting traditional college and university foreign language curriculum. By making foreign language instruction available from the earliest grade levels and in public schools, at no direct cost to students and their families, the campaign for foreign languages is potentially disruptive to elite private schools who have often provided this advantage to a small percentage of students, to colleges and universities which often provide only introductory language classes, followed by advanced courses generally in literature and literary studies, and to commercial language schools, which have contributed to the commodification of language skills. As in any successful grassroots political campaign, the campaign for foreign languages relies on getting the message out directly and personally to families and communities, using authentic and genuine communication, in addition to more institutional types of outreach.

Successful Grassroots Political Campaigns

While educational in nature, the campaign for foreign languages is also a grassroots political campaign, and needs to incorporate the strategies and tactics of successful grassroots campaigns – the need to focus on the people most likely to actively support the cause; the need to select the people who will be talking to the community and who are most likely to be able to make the case for languages; the need to listen to what the community is saying; the need to focus on people, and not just on technology; and the need to measure and assess what is actually impactful.

The Role of Blue Ocean Strategy

Blue ocean strategy, as described by Kim and Mauborgne, emphasizes the development of new markets, rather than their competition. In the case of the campaign for foreign languages, it is not difficult to envision underserved populations including people already in the workforce as potential "blue ocean" new markets. The underlying principle of blue ocean strategy is value innovation, which brings value to the buyer or consumer (student and community) through differentiation of the product or service offered at a lower cost. Key elements of blue ocean strategy include creating an uncontested market space, making the competition irrelevant, creating and capturing new demand, breaking the value-cost trade-off, and – most importantly -- aligning the whole system of the organization in pursuit of differentiation and low cost.

Kim and Mauborgne develop the concept of blue ocean strategy further as a blue ocean shift, outlining the actual steps required and describing the three key components of a successful blue ocean shift: adopting a blue ocean perspective, having practical tools for market creation, and having humanistic processes and values.

However, the key to success in a highly competitive world, where educational institutions face financial challenges, and where school subjects and disciplines are at times competitors for limited funds in a zero-sum environment, is blue ocean strategy. The strategy empowers a paradigm shift in favor of foreign languages by seeking out blue ocean markets, aka, parents, communities, and learners themselves who have never actively considered foreign languages as part of the essential skills set in a globalized marketplace and globalized world.

Rather than competing with other departments for scarce resources, a campaign for foreign languages driven by blue ocean strategy will create demand for foreign languages where none existed before, mobilize parents and community leaders to advocate for foreign languages within their schools and school districts, and provide value by offering a pathway, not only to multilingualism, but to academic and career success, for learners and communities, and for schools seeking to differentiate themselves qualitatively.

Figure 1. The Campaign for Foreign Languages

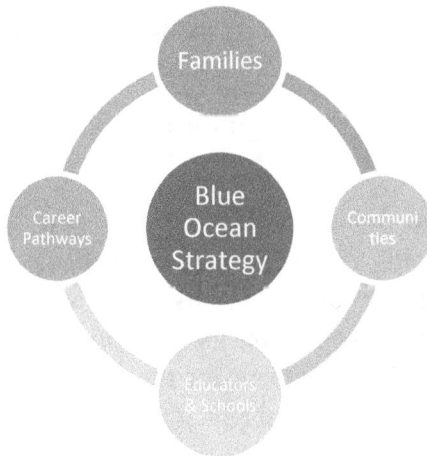

Figure 2. Blue Ocean Strategy - The Campaign for Foreign Languages

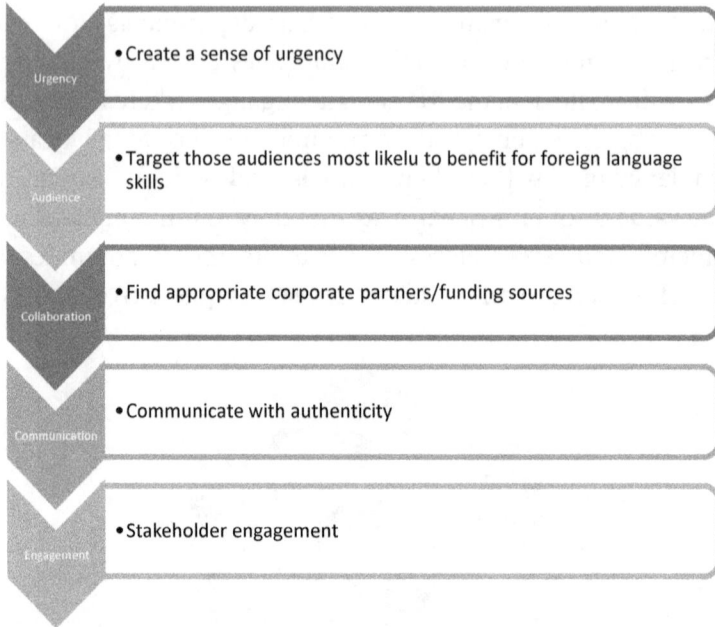

Urgency
- Create a sense of urgency

Audience
- Target those audiences most likelu to benefit for foreign language skills

Collaboration
- Find appropriate corporate partners/funding sources

Communication
- Communicate with authenticity

Engagement
- Stakeholder engagement

Figure 3. Blue Ocean Action Steps for Foreign Languages

While bringing about a paradigm shift of this magnitude is never easy, it is important to remember that we can all be change agents – in our families, communities, schools, and beyond. Every paradigm shift begins with one person. It can begin today with each one of us as bilingual parents and foreign language advocates.

The Campaign for Foreign Languages

As already discussed, the business case for foreign language learning pertains not only to the benefits that accrue to foreign language learners, but -- just as importantly -- foreign language advocates must adapt the business theories and methodologies used by business and government for the purpose of the developing an effective and strategic campaign.

In addition to change management, social marketing, cause marketing, disruptive innovation, psychology of influence and science of persuasion, and -- most importantly -- blue ocean strategy, lobbying and Six Sigma should also be considered as potential campaign tools.

Lobbying

Lobbying has been defined as "attempting to influence business and government leaders." A complex task in itself, lobbying appears even more complicated due to the fact that, in addition to registered lobbyists, many other professionals in government affairs, public affairs, public relations, consulting, and even professional and trade associations, etc. may actually perform a similar function.

In a broader sense, all of us who support and advocate for a cause -- in this case, foreign language education -- as change agents, could be considered citizen lobbyists. It is for that reason that it is useful to consider how professional, registered lobbyists go about their task of influencing business and government leaders to take actions and pass legislation that favors a particular cause or idea.

While we have already discussed the nature and importance of the psychology of influence and the science of persuasion in developing an effective campaign for foreign languages, lobbying lends a pragmatic perspective on the process, and effective lobbyists -- including all of us who are citizen change agents/lobbyists -- must keep in mind practical and procedural practices in addition to remaining focused on the big idea, or big picture of what we are promoting and advocating for the greater good. It is important also to remember that lobbying business organizations and government officials is only a subset of the mission of an effective advocate for foreign language learning, with families, communities, and the future of our children being the heart of the mission.

A recent article on the habits of an effective lobbyist stresses the importance of clearly identifying oneself, being polite and professional, having a clear and concise message, making it personal by conveying why the issue of foreign language learning is important to each one of us personally, being accurate and truthful, being prepared to work with government and legislative staff when officials may be challenging to schedule time with, being prepared to compromise if necessary, being willing to engage in dialogue with officials and staffers, using online and social media appropriately, and thanking all those who have helped and supported our cause (Makarian).

Among the qualities that make for a good lobbyist, subject matter expertise, knowledge of the relevant individuals and organizations, knowledge of legislative processes and procedures, people skills, sound judgment, political savvy, and excellent communication skills are frequently mentioned. However, timing and patience are essential to effective advocacy and lobbying (Lebov).

Although many groups and individuals advocate for foreign languages, JNCL-NCLIS is considered the sole actual lobbyist for foreign languages in the United States.

Challenges to the use of the term "lobby," in connection with foreign languages, include negative connotations from the press in terms of lack of integrity and transparency. However, a case can be made that lobbying can bring about reform and positive change, can bring together different groups, can influence both public opinion and government policy and action, and can provide information on specific issues to policymakers and decision makers. If corporations and big business use lobbying in order to achieve their goals, then good causes can and should do so as well.

It is important to consider lobbying from the perspective of bringing about positive change through increasing awareness of a cause or issue–in this case, foreign language learning–and providing information to legislators and other policy makers. Lobbying for the cause can be an important part of the campaign for foreign languages.

Six Sigma and Lean Six Sigma

The term "Six Sigma" is often used in terms of process improvement and data-driven management, and it is important to consider how this strategy can be utilized to improve the campaign for foreign languages. The core value that drives Six Sigma is developing a process, in this case the campaign for foreign language learning. The tools of Six Sigma are commonly referred to as DMAIC -- define, measure, analyze, improve, and control. In the case of foreign language learning in the United States, it would be necessary to define the problem, the lack of foreign language skills among English-speaking Americans. Once defined, the dimensions of the United States foreign language deficit would be quantified and analyzed to determine causes and challenges, strategies would be developed to respond to the problem and to improve foreign language learning, and metrics would be developed to monitor progress.

The primary contribution of Six Sigma to the issue of increasing foreign language skills lies in its emphasis on problem solving and developing a strategy before implementing tactics. In many cases, foreign language advocacy is tactics-driven, responding to crises as they occur, rather than developing a long-term measurable strategy for positive change.

The term Lean Six Sigma is often used, combining the principles of lean management with the process improvement of Six Sigma. The primary contribution of consideration of Lean Six Sigma is the lack of resources, both financial and personnel, associated with any campaign for foreign languages, where funding depends largely on member contributions and where staffing is provided by individual volunteer change agents who are also very busy teachers and educators. For these reasons, any campaign strategy that would maximize return on either investment of funds or of personal time and effort would benefit the campaign greatly.

For example, in terms of maximizing the impact of the scant personal and financial resources that characterize the campaign for foreign language learning, it would be revelatory to examine the impact of a social media campaign versus the presence of foreign language advocates at public meetings of a Board of Education or Board of Trustees where foreign language education is to be discussed. While it is tempting to think that social media might have a broader reach with less time and effort, or conversely, that a personal presence of foreign language advocates at a meeting would be impactful, only the results and data will confirm which tactic is likely to yield a better result.

Strategic Foreign Language Advocacy

So many foreign language educators are doing wonderful work in their classrooms and schools, as well as in a wide range of professional development and advocacy initiatives. In addition, foreign language supporters and advocates are also to be found in our families and communities, as well as in private enterprise and among our elected and public officials.

Foreign language advocacy is both institutional and personal, with advocacy efforts led by our professional associations and other groups, as well as by concerned parents and individuals from all walks of life who believe in the importance of language learning for the individual and for our society.

The lack of foreign language skills in the United States negatively impacts our economic and national security. That being said, in an increasing globalized world and multilingual America, fewer than 20% of K-12 public school students are studying a foreign language, and at the college and university level, only 7.5% of students are enrolled in a course in a language other than English.

Among the challenges that may face foreign language advocacy and advocates, a frequent, but frustrating, occurrence is the announcement that a foreign language program is being cut, or even eliminated. As these announcements are often made at the end of the school/academic year, sometimes coinciding with the retirement or departure of a respected teacher, and effective by the beginning of the new school/academic year, there is little time to react and to organize a campaign to save the affected program what would have any likelihood of success. A few letters hastily written or signed as classes are ending are unlikely to change the mind of the administrator who has made the decision, and may even make things worse for the program, and possibly for the campaign organizer.

Strategic Foreign Language Advocacy

The strategy to strengthen, to protect, and to defend our foreign language programs is proactive foreign language advocacy, which begins from the first day, and continues on an ongoing basis when a program is strong and successful. This type of advocacy is intended to develop a local network of support for the program within the school and community, and to -- hopefully -- avoid any thought of cutbacks or elimination.

A strategy of ongoing proactive advocacy can and should use both traditional, as well as online social media methods, and needs to target students, parents, alumni, and school administrators, as well as current and potential partners in the community and in the wider local and regional committee. An effective strategy would certainly highlight the achievements of students, while demonstrating the personal, social, and professional advantages of foreign language skills and cultural knowledge.

Figure 4. Strategic Foreign Language Advocacy

Another challenge is that students sometimes come to the realization that they actually want or need to learn another language only when an opportunity for a study away experience or internship appears, and there is little preparation time. In addition, students are often motivated to make the world a better place, but do not have the language skills and cultural knowledge needed to be effective global citizens in a multilingual world.

A third challenge is that some foreign language supporters may feel that, while they support foreign language learning for a particular purpose, they may hesitate to become associated with a broad-based institutional-type campaign but would prefer a niche-style campaign focusing on a specific language, grade level(s), methodology, or purpose.

Other foreign language supporters may prefer a purely online or social media campaign, willing to sign online petitions, while other may prefer face-to-face meetings and discussion. Yet others may feel that, due to family, job, and other commitments, they do not have time to actively participate, but are willing to donate to, or vote for, a cause.

The good news is that strategic foreign language advocacy, as a concept, is far from "one size fits all," but rather is a broad-based coalition that wants and needs all our support, whether as part of a funded organizational campaign, or as a grassroots community activist, either online or on site.

The Strategic Foreign Language Advocacy Plan

Development and implementation of a plan for strategic foreign language advocacy should stem from the interests and abilities of the participants, and the time, money, and technology available. The first step is to create a "buzz" about foreign languages and present foreign language learning as cool, hip, and trendy. The methods can include online and social media posts, as well as face-to-face programming and events highlighting the advantages of foreign language skills and featuring celebrities (local "celebrities," too!), entertainment, food, etc., with the specifics individualized to local needs and the target audience.

Another element in creating and sustaining a "buzz" about foreign languages is the selective dissemination of information to classroom teachers and other supporters who may not have the time to systematically search for this needed information on a regular basis.

In addition to promoting foreign languages and sharing information, foreign language educators should work within their professional associations to develop opportunities to showcase foreign language skills and to take advantage of all that currently exists. Developing local programs, events, and contests to showcase students' foreign language skills and to seek external funding is another possible action step. Local experiential learning and volunteer opportunities, and showcasing foreign language learners, are also a way to enhance the perception of foreign languages.

While this step is not difficult, the challenge is in developing and sustaining motivation in people to learn a foreign language rather than devote that same time and energy to develop some other skill. However, creating and maintaining a "buzz" about foreign languages is essential to develop sustainable foreign language learning.

Being Present in the Community

In addition to working to create a buzz about foreign languages, the strategic foreign language advocate needs to be present and active within the educational institution and in the local community, possibly sponsoring free and informal language events like language tables at the library or community center, where learners and heritage speakers can come together.

It is also important for the strategic foreign language advocate to maintain a dialogue with local education administrators and public officials, keeping them informed about the exciting things happening in the foreign language classroom. While face-to-face meetings and classroom visits are wonderful, an online newsletter is an excellent alternative.

It is most important for an effective strategic foreign language advocate to participate in professional and related foreign language education associations, to take appropriate leadership roles and/or to write for practitioner and research publications, and to speak at conferences, etc. Political engagement, whether as a voter, supporter, or candidate is another method of supporting foreign language education.

Being present in the local and educational community may serve to forewarn educators and communities that cuts in foreign languages and potential eliminations are being considered, discussed, or even planned.

Re-Booting Endangered and Eliminated Programs

When you realize that your program is in danger, it is often too late. If a decision has already been made to cut or to eliminate a program, it is difficult to change that decision. Even if a proposed cut or elimination is on the table, it indicates some level of support of that idea among administrators and decision-makers, and again, it is very difficult to bring people to let go of "their" idea. It is far better to strategically and proactively avoid any consideration or discussion of any cut or elimination.

However, even when this occurs, it is necessary "to fight the good fight," reaching out to both present and potential allies and supporters at the local, state, regional, and national levels, and using social media and online petitions in addition to in-person advocacy. While this may or may not save your program, it may serve as a deterrent to further cuts.

It is even more difficult to bring back a program that has been eliminated, especially as many program eliminations occur after the retirement or departure of a respected foreign language educator, and budget is often cited as the reason. However, it is not impossible to bring back a program -- gradually, with a part-time teacher, or as a minor, double major, or interdisciplinary program (at the college and university level), in a cost-sharing arrangement with another institution, or an online program that may not even originate locally. As success is, by no means, certain in the process of reviving a program that has been eliminated, foreign language supporters will need to work together, and to remain vigilant to any new threats, for some time.

The Individual Change Agent

Every paradigm shift starts with one person. Creating a new program is possibly the most daunting challenge for the strategic foreign language advocate, as there is no structure in place, no budget, no history, no network of supporters, and possibly not even a perceived need of a new language program.

However, it is not impossible. Many educational decisions are made locally -- in the school or school district, or on a college or university campus. A strategic foreign language advocate convinced of the need for a new language program needs to build a grassroots coalition of supporters who share the same vision and to make the case to school administrators and to decision-makers, using all of the strategies and tactics of an effective campaign, and present a reasonable case grounded in the existing research on the benefits of foreign language skills. This is also where local "celebrities," community leaders and groups who speak the target language(s), can be valuable supporters and allies.

L'union fait la force

It is, above all, essential for foreign language educators to work together, and to work with fellow foreign language stakeholders in the community, in the private sector, and in government.

Strategic foreign language advocacy encompasses different languages and different approaches and methodologies. It cannot be considered a zero-sum equation, where one program can only win if another loses. Traditional and immersion foreign language educators, teachers of different languages, and K-16 educators need to stand together, as *l'union fait la force!*

Chapter 6

A Pathway to Effective Foreign Language Learning

Foreign languages are quintessentially interdisciplinary. As the key component of human communication, languages reflect the entire scope of the human experience. The significance of this innate interdisciplinarity and its consequences in foreign language learning are inescapable.

The foreign language teacher is, by definition, the teacher of the culture of those who speak the target language and all that it entails -- literature, of course, but also history, art, music, politics, lifestyle, and much more. Reflecting the European Union's core value of multilingualism, Michael Byram has written extensively on the role of foreign languages in intercultural communication, intercultural competence, and intercultural citizenship, and Lies Sercu has written on foreign language learning, describing the foreign language teacher as an intercultural competence teacher. In the United States, the MLA report, *Foreign Languages and Higher Education: New Structures for a Changed World* emphasizes the importance of translingual and transcultural competence, and the importance of the leadership role of foreign language educators in K-16 collaborative partnerships.

There are so many ways to learn other languages -- from our families and communities, in the workplace, and in the classroom or online learning environment. However, most Americans who study another language do so in a classroom environment, whether face-to-face, online, or in a hybrid learning environment. Beyond that, the question of how to learn, driven by why we are learning another language, can lead to multiple pathways.

Often, language learning can focus on grammar and vocabulary, which -- although essential -- can lack the authenticity and cultural and communicative context that bring meaning to the process and sustain the foreign language learner through the inevitable plateaus in language learning. Authentic media and texts can help to sustain motivation, but the question arises as to which authentic materials, and for which learners. In the earlier grade levels and levels of language learning, it is easy to envision social, school, and family topics that would be applicable to all or most language learners, but as students advance, reaching the final years of high school, and the college and university level studies, interests become even more widely divergent, with discipline-based and discipline-related authentic materials becoming more important, and even essential, to sustain motivation.

A business or science student may have different goals and objectives in life and in language learning than a humanities or social sciences student. Authentic materials and experiences in foreign language learning need to echo these disciplinary interests, as well as the many varied personal interests of young adult learners. Course content, readings, and experiential learning can offer a pathway to language learning in an interdisciplinary context, and studies related to global, international, and regional issues can call for readings, media, and experiences in the target language and culture. Study away and study abroad can complement classroom and online learning, but it is important to provide a variety of platforms for residency experiences, including short- and medium-term experiences accessible to a broader cross-section of students than the traditional semester or year abroad. These shorter-term experiences can also be more specific to students in a particular discipline or major.

Another way to achieve interdisciplinarity in foreign language learning is the double major, which empowers students to pursue a career or professionally-oriented degree program while continuing language learning in the second major. Team-teaching, and courses in the first major that allow an additional module to examine materials in a second language are among best practices.

While the 2007 MLA report, *Foreign Languages and Higher Education*, called for translingual and transcultural competence, colleges and universities have created interdisciplinary foreign language learning opportunities through Languages for Specific Purposes (LSP) and Business Language Studies (BLS), as well as through active development and promotion of double major opportunities. In addition, pre-professional and area studies-type programs offer a pathway to careers in language services, international relations, global and international studies, etc.

The Challenge of Language Proficiency

While certain programs at the undergraduate and graduate level have taken the initiative in offering possibilities for integrating majors across the disciplines with foreign language study and even with a second major in one or more foreign languages, the true challenge lies in the lack of foreign language skills among many college and university students who would like to have the foreign language and intercultural skills necessary to make a difference in the world as global citizens.

Although colleges and universities offer a wide array of foreign language courses, the challenge is that college and university students -- for many reasons, including cost, the pressure of courses in their majors, etc. -- cannot begin foreign language study, or even continue high school foreign language studies in college.

The real challenge is to provide all/most students with the opportunity for foreign language study in the early grades so that -- when they get to the college and university campus -- they have proficiency to do the things that they want to with languages: to do international fieldwork; to conduct international business; and more importantly, to effectively address global issues in a multilingual and multilcultural world and workplace.

Action Steps Moving Forward

It is important for foreign language educators to build relationships within the community to advocate for and to support foreign language learning, in order to build proficiency and even fluency from the earliest grade levels through traditional, heritage, and immersion foreign language programs. It is also important to provide for the creation of authentic learning materials and the training and professional development of foreign language teachers.

Most importantly, it is important to increase awareness within the community of the benefits and advantages of foreign language skills, and to deploy the best in theory and practice in change management and blue ocean strategy, in order to increase both awareness and opportunity for foreign language learning.

Methods of Teaching Foreign Languages

People decide to learn a foreign language for many different reasons, and at different times in their lives. In addition, people have different interests and learning styles, so teaching a foreign language cannot and has never been a "one-size-fits-all" approach. Methods of teaching foreign languages have changed and evolved over time, reflecting changes in modern life, new and evolving linguistic theories, and in response to best practices. Much current teaching involves language as communication and an expression of culture, and has been inspired by the concepts of translingual and transcultural competence as articulated in the MLA report, *Foreign Languages and Higher Education: New Structures for a Changed World.*

If a graduate student is learning another language in order to read scholarly articles, his/her language needs are different than if a worker is learning another language to work with international co-workers or customers. If a student is learning another language out of interest, or to prepare for study abroad, his/her language needs are different than if a student is fulfilling a language requirement for college admission or college graduation. Some learners may want to learn a language through its great literature, while others would prefer non-fiction books, film, or vocal music. Some learners prefer reading and writing, others prefer speaking and listening. Some learn better while sitting quietly, while others learn better while performing a physical activity, alone or with others. The best teaching method is always the one best suited to the needs and desires of the learner.

While, traditionally, students have learned a foreign language in a classroom, students now have access to online technology, media, and social media, as they learn another language, whether they are in a traditional classroom setting, or whether they are in a wholly online program. The obvious advantage is that the student who lives at a distance from a school or college campus, or the student who is not able to travel or study for a variety of reasons, can still experience authentic language and mother tongue speakers.

Selected Teaching Methodologies

Teaching methods may be based on a theory of language learning. Traditional methods, using various terminologies, have stressed grammar, vocabulary, writing, structured drills and repetition, structured conversation, and translation, and courses have often been textbook-driven. As immersion is generally considered to have the most likelihood of successful learning outcome, in more recent years, methods have included CLIL, CBI, TPR, TPRS, CI, and more. These methods emphasize the importance of remaining as much as possible in the target language in order to enhance proficiency as well as the importance of natural and authentic learning experiences that mirror as closely as possible the experience of learning our mother tongue. The most important thing is that the method be the right one for the learner, considering the goals, linguistic background, and the learning and cognitive style of the learner.

CLIL (Content and Language Integrated Learning), is a term frequently associated with Europe, where the language is the medium of instruction in a subject class, where the emphasis remains on the subject matter being taught as also a means of learning the language through the learner's interest in the subject.

CBI (Content-Based Instruction) is similar to the use of L1 and L2 for different subjects in an immersion program, where the language is used as a medium of instruction for specific subjects, with students able to learn the language in a natural manner and setting, using the learner's interest in the subject as a means to increasing language learning motivation and outcomes.

TPR (Total Physical Response) uses physical movement and activity to launch language learning, and TPRS (Teaching Proficiency through Reading and Storytelling) builds on TPR to teach more complex and abstract terms and concepts that cannot be taught or learned through TPR alone. While it empowers higher-level thought and expression of ideas, it builds on physical activity to expand the concept to include storytelling, writing, etc.

CI (Comprehensible Input), often associated with the theories of linguist Stephen Krashen, is grounded in the idea that mother tongue language learning often takes place when the child understands most of what is being said, and guesses or infers the rest, using contextual clues, etc., and tries to mirror that experience in second language learning, where a text or conversation will be just slightly above the level of the learner, encouraging learner progress toward proficiency.

The most important thing is that the method be the right one for the learner, and one of the most important factors to consider is the age of the learner. Adult learners, who may be studying another language for a variety of reasons, may approach learning differently from children, and andragogy is the term often used to describe and explain the learning needs of adults. While adult learners tend to be goal-oriented and relatively self-aware in terms of their language abilities, they often have less time for classes and study due to family, work, and other commitments, and they may have already had a less than successful language learning experience while in school. It is important for the instructor to take all of these factors into consideration when planning classes and assignments and also equally important to maintain a high level of expectations, and to make every effort to keep the sessions enjoyable, interesting and relevant.

Developing Sustainable
Language Learning Motivation

However, while the methodology used by the foreign language educator is important, it is also important to look at the learner side of the equation, and most specifically, learner motivation. One of the issues in foreign language in the United States concerns the lack of motivation among English-speaking Americans to begin, or to even consider, foreign language study, and fewer than 20% of K-12 public school students, and just over 7% of college and university students, are actually studying another language. While highly educated and skilled foreign language educators are effectively deploying a range of carefully thought out methodologies in the classroom, the professionalism and dedication of foreign language educators are not even reaching the vast majority of American students.

In terms of a student actually choosing to learn another language, their perseverance through the relatively long process of language learning, and their eventual success as language learners, motivation is essential and often problematic when English-speakers view their mother tongue as the global *lingua franca* and fail to see any reason to study another language.

When discussing motivation to learn a language, the terms "instrumental motivation" and "integrative motivation" are often used, with "instrumental motivation" referring to motivation that is goal-oriented, as in fulfilling a language requirement in school, or earning a promotion or pay increase in the workplace, and "integrative motivation" describing language learning as an extension of personal interest in another culture. Of the two, integrative motivation is the more closely associated with language learning success.

If the United States is to overcome its foreign language deficit and enjoy the social, cultural, economic, and global benefits associated with multilingualism, and the number of Americans learning other languages is to increase, then integrative motivation to begin and to continue foreign language learning needs to be developed and sustained.

Parents, communities, foreign language advocates, and language stakeholders need to work to develop interest in other cultures and their languages -- integrative motivation -- from the earliest age, and to continue to work together to support foreign language educators as they effectively utilize an array of teaching methodologies and materials to sustain motivation so that the young generation can reach proficiency and so that our society can become truly bilingual.

Chapter 7

The Potential of Dual-Language
Education

A s Francois Grosjean famously stated: "Bilinguals are those who use two or more languages (or dialects) in their daily lives." In the United States, many bilinguals have grown up speaking another language in the home. As a result, many Americans consider that being bilingual actually means to speak another language perfectly, without accent, and with mother tongue fluency. However, that may not be a truly complete definition of what it means to be bilingual, as people around the world may use one or more additional languages in the workplace, at school, in the home, in the community, and when searching for or consuming news, information, and entertainment through print, online and broadcast media. It is not an all-or-nothing learning proposition.

Bilingual people may have varying degrees of skill and fluency in each of their different languages, depending on when and how they first learned it, and how they use it. For example, a bilingual who learned a language at a later age, and who uses it primarily passively -- reading and listening, may retain an accent in conversation, while a bilingual who learned another language as a child in the home may speak without an accent, but may not have business or technical language skills in the language. Just as individuals may use their mother tongue differently, bilingual language skills vary.

It is important for American language learners and prospective learners to understand that learning goals are different depending on the intended use of the new language -- as an occasional versus everyday user, as a recreational versus a workplace user, or if the plan

93

is to study abroad for a degree or advanced degree where the target language is also the medium of instruction. Having scaffolded and realistic expectations makes the language learning process less daunting and can also help to avoid discouragement and perhaps abandonment of language learning during the more difficult stages and during the inevitable plateaus. The European concept of plurilingualism is closer to this idea, with its realistic expectations, and could perhaps be adapted to the conversation on language learning and multilingualism in the United States.

Why is Multilingualism Important?

Multilingualism impacts the whole person, providing personal, cultural, professional, and societal benefits. Personal benefits include both cognitive and academic benefits. The regular use of more than one language has been shown to stave off the onset of dementia, to improve decision-making and problem-solving, and has been associated with tolerance and creativity, as well as with better test scores and academic outcomes,

Cultural advantages include the ability to enjoy literature, film, and vocal music in the original, and to access news and media reflecting perhaps a different perspective and worldview. Travel may also replace simple tourism, as interactions with locals, in the local language, become possible.

As language is a social and communicative skill, being bilingual also opens the door to interactions with members of the local community who may express themselves more easily in another language, and if the additional language is a heritage language, it opens the door to an entirely different level of understanding of one's family background and of one's own personal cultural identity.

Multilingualism is important in the workplace whether an individual is seeking an international, perhaps expatriate, career, whether one works for a multinational corporation or organization, whether one works for a company or organization that has clients or customers outside the United States, or whether the local community served by a company or organization in the United States has a significant number of speakers of another language.

Professional advantages include the ability to communicate with co-workers and clients/customers in the local language, and in cases where the official corporate or organizational language may be English, many of the side conversations and social interactions are likely to be in the local language.

The benefits of multilingualism extend to companies and organizations as well, as diversity has been associated with more rational decision-making and more effective problem-solving. Multinational companies know first-hand that fluency in languages is essential to communicate and understand managers, customers, and consumers around the world. To achieve this, knowing languages is essential.

The societal benefits of multilingualism include local, national, and global benefits, as the United States is and always has been a multilingual and multicultural nation, and understanding and acceptance of other cultures is a cornerstone of US history. Communication with, and understanding of, other linguistic and cultural groups can only result in a more harmonious society.

Beyond the local and national benefits, knowledge of other languages and cultures has been linked to international understanding and global citizenship. Discussion, decision-making, and problem-solving of complex global issues are improved when numerous stakeholders, representing many languages, are part of the process. For this reason, the UN has 6 official languages, and many other international organizations have official languages and language policies. It is noteworthy that the United Nations Academic Impact launched the Many Languages One World Essay Contest and Global Youth Forum in 2013 in order to highlight the significance of multilingualism in global citizenship, bringing college and university student contest winners to New York, all expenses paid, to present in a learned second language on the UN Sustainable Development Goals (SDGs) in the General Assembly Hall of the UN.

Building Bilingual Communities

Often the question is asked whether multilingualism will weaken a country. There are a number of examples of nation states that are officially bilingual and/or have more than one language that are prevalent in daily life, with little apparent risk. On the contrary, the example that immediately comes to mind is Canada, which is an especially interesting case for a host of reasons. In addition to bordering the United States and sharing our North American context, Canada is a major trading partner of the United States. That being said, Canada differs from the United States in a multitude of ways, perhaps most significantly in its policy of official bilingualism in English and French, which has existed in its current form for the past half century. An interesting aspect of Canadian bilingualism is that the current half-century of bilingualism follows Quebec's two centuries of relative isolation from France. Not only has French endured, many would say that it has thrived despite its isolation, with demand for French language immersion across Canada from both francophone and non-francophone parents outpacing the supply of teachers. In addition, Montreal has been ranked the most attractive city for international students, precisely because university degrees at all levels are available in more than one language, in English and in French. As both English and French are among the top three languages for international business, with two of the three as official languages, Canada may well have an advantage over the United States.

While the potential economic impact of multilingualism is often mentioned, it is interesting to note that Switzerland, another country with more than one official language (three official languages,

French, German, and Italian, plus an additional national language, Romansch) is ranked #1 in the *Global Competitiveness Index*, followed by the United States in second place. In terms of global competitiveness, Switzerland ranked #1 in 2017-2018, with the United States just behind, at #2.

It is overwhelmingly clear that -- for reasons of economic and national security, as well as for reasons of personal, professional, and societal benefits, building foreign language skills is important for our society, for each of us personally, and -- most importantly -- for our children, for the current and the next generation.

The question really is: how?

In the face of widespread reluctance to learn foreign languages in the United States, it is really necessary for foreign language educators, advocates, stakeholders, and supporters to take a proactive and vigorous approach, acting jointly through professional and related associations, but also individually -- as change agents, in the family and community, through online and social media, and in the broader public conversation, speaking out in support of foreign languages and winning people over one at a time, with the urgency of the issue for our children, our communities, and our world.

With the benefits of multilingualism and multiliteracy becoming clearer to researchers—in particular the impact of multilingualism on cognitive enhancement, critical thinking, and sensitivity toward other people and cultures—it is equally important that we find ways to inspire and engage all parents to become language advocates. These individuals will not just be advocates of dual-language education, but true pioneers willing to spur positive change in their societies and re-enchant the public with public schools, all the while promoting an active community life (socially, economically, culturally) and a mutual understanding and respect for minority groups and people of varying sociolinguistic and economic backgrounds. This is the path to break the crippling cycle whereby access to good education is often linked to household income and status.

The Goals of Dual-Language Immersion

According to the Center for Applied Linguistics (CAL), "the goals of dual language are for students to develop high levels of language proficiency and literacy in both program languages, to demonstrate high levels of academic achievement, and to develop an appreciation for and an understanding of diverse cultures."

The decision-making process of a community, school district, and of the family of a student is logically focused on the benefits of multilingualism for the learner and for the community, and by extension, our society.

It is well known that the personal and professional benefits of foreign language skills include cultural and cognitive advantages, creativity, as well as potentially increased earnings and employability, and that students in immersion programs tend to demonstrate higher levels of academic achievement. However, the social, sociocultural, and societal benefits of multilingualism are not always as frequently considered and discussed.

While it is relatively simple for any interested person to learn about the outward manifestations of a culture -- holidays, festivals, food, music, dance, traditional costumes, etc., it is exponentially more difficult to learn the underlying values and beliefs of a culture. Learning about the visible culture, or the tip of the "cultural iceberg," a metaphor made famous by the anthropologist Edward T. Hall, needs to lead to learning about the more hidden aspects of the culture if true intercultural understanding is to develop.

Foreign language teachers have often considered themselves intercultural competence teachers, and the MLA has defined translingual and transcultural competence as the goals of foreign language learning. However, immersion education, where another language is learned at a relatively early age, and particularly dual-language immersion, where native speakers of both languages are present, offers the best opportunity for students to acquire cultural competence, along with the communicative skills of language.

While foreign language skills are certainly a first step in learning about another cultural heritage, whether in a traditional or immersion foreign language class, interacting with mother-tongue speakers -- as is the norm in a dual-language immersion environment -- as the learner is developing language and communicative skills, is an infinitely more effective method of developing intercultural competence.

By learning language and culture from a young age in a DLI classroom, students can develop the language skills and intercultural knowledge needed for travel, study abroad, transnational careers, and in order to effectively navigate our own increasingly multilingual society.

In addition, both linguistic skills and cultural knowledge form part of the global skills set needed if young people are to be able to both participate in and enjoy the cultures of the world and to accept their role and responsibilities as global citizens capable of addressing complex global issues with an understanding of divergent worldviews.

At present, more and more bilingual or multilingual streams are being created, both for English learners and for English speakers for whom English is the first language. This is partly explained by the fact that teaching languages to children makes them more competitive in a global economy. In addition, it strengthens their ability to learn other foreign languages, to listen better in class, to have better reading skills and even to have better results in mathematics. These streams allow students to benefit from multilingualism, regardless of the language skills they originally inherited.

In recent years, these streams have evolved towards a language education model that focuses more on the benefits of multilingualism for children who may or may not speak another language, rather than the needs of immigrants.

The bilingual streams of the United States exist in many languages. If English is still one of the two languages, we find courses in Spanish, Chinese, Korean, French, Japanese, German, Russian, Portuguese, Arabic, Italian, Cantonese, Hmong, Bengali, Urdu, Creole, Cup'ik or Ojibwe, to name a few. You can even find a bilingual stream in American Sign Language. Each of these languages reflects the spirit of the community surrounding the language–its diversity, its interests, and its shared desire to make its children successful. By creating these channels, each community contributes to making the United States more competitive in both education and economics.

Dual-language education means different things to different people. Some want access to English and the equal opportunity it provides. Others want to sustain their heritage and utilize dual-language education as a tool to do so. Others are interested in the benefits of multilingualism for cognitive development. Others are interested in the acquisition of a second, third, or fourth language because of the professional opportunities and advantages it will yield. Ultimately, these perspectives share the same goal: to create a multilingual society with greater access to languages and cultures.

Multilingual education in the United States has many facets. No federal law regulates academic content. Each school district is in charge of its own pedagogy, while standards are set at the state level. However, the number and variety of language streams may surprise parents and educators who would like to introduce such programs into their communities.

It is critical that we try to weave together these different perspectives, ensuring that more dual-language programs are created to generate greater opportunities for all children. Being bilingual is no longer superfluous nor the privilege of a happy few. Being bilingual is no longer taboo for immigrants who want so dearly for their children to blend seamlessly into their new environment. Being bilingual is the new norm, and it must start with our youngest citizens.

Foreign language skills have many benefits, including personal, social, and cultural benefits, as well as professional, career, and workplace benefits. Knowledge and use of more than one language have been linked to creativity (Kharkhurin, 2012; European Commission, 2009), problem-solving (Academy of Finland, 2009), being a better employee/worker (Hogan-Brun, 2017), and to mental acuity (Bialystok, 2012). Language skills and cultural knowledge enhance human capital and provide economic and social benefits. In addition, foreign language skills and knowledge of other cultures play a significant role in the development of a global mindset and values of global citizenship (Gunesch, 2008).

Multilingualism is increasingly an essential skill. International trade and globalization have added to the multilingual advantage, and business organizations need a language strategy to effectively manage language skills and cultural knowledge as global talent. The reality is that 75% of the world population does not speak English (British Council, 2013), which represents a tremendous opportunity for multilingual individuals. Additionally, a growing percentage of the largest global organizations, with employee bases numbering in the tens of millions, are not located in the predominantly English-speaking world.

Not only has globalization resulted in a more interconnected world, but in the United States, the millions of citizens who speak a language other than English in the home make it more important than ever to look to the significance of diversity both in the world and in our communities. Reducing social segmentation, broadening the base, and creating an environment of inclusivity, can indeed increase opportunities, openness, and societal well-being.

Just as multilingualism has been linked to creativity and problem-solving in the individual, diversity -- including linguistic diversity -- has been linked to creativity and problem-solving in transnational and multilingual teams (Livermore, 2016; Florida, 2008; Elgar,

2014). These are not, as they are often incorrectly labeled, "soft skills." Rather, they represent critical business skills of cross-cultural communication necessary to succeed and grow in a multicultural and multilingual world.

A common language has been linked to increased trade and GDP within the EU and within the Francophonie (FERDI, n.d.). In Britain, Canada, Switzerland, and the EU, language skills have been linked both to higher earnings and to employability and continued employment, even in the face of increased costs.

Multilingualism, supported and driven by foreign language advocacy, also creates economic growth and opportunity. Multilingual individuals, whether in the Americas, Africa, Europe, or Asia have increased economic mobility, and reduced opportunity costs when leaving one location for another. Creating this rich tapestry of multilingual ideas, people, and culture provides the foundation for innovation that nations, corporations, and individuals see as keys to sustainable success.

A robust and comprehensive foreign language advocacy policy can address these challenges. Effective advocacy should strive to provide opportunity to begin foreign language study at an early age, and to support continued study of one or more languages to proficiency, or even fluency. To accomplish this goal, we need to pursue a policy that is resolutely favorable to multilingualism by affirming the importance of each student's mastery of two foreign languages. There are great examples to borrow from, starting with the recommendations of the European Union, which called for continued efforts to "improve the mastery of basic skills, including the teaching of at least two foreign languages from a very early age" (Barcelona, 2002, in European Commission, 2012).

The main reforms that have marked the educational landscape since, in 2013, 2016 and 2017, have been in line with the 2006 Renovation Plan. They have reinforced the place of languages in the essential foundation of learning, emphasized the importance of oral communication and promoted more and more early education. The common foundation of knowledge, skills and culture, renovated in 2016, includes language learning in language area.

The key to success is an advocacy partnership among educators, parents, and other foreign language stakeholders, and it is important to highlight the personal, social, workplace, and economic benefits of multilingualism and multiliteracy. With support including, but not limited to, leading multinational organizations, global NGOs, and prestigious business publications such as the *Harvard Business Review*, the case is clear. The future of success, and of succeeding as a person, corporation, or nation, is in multilingualism.

Chapter 8

The Global Significance of Multilingualism

Although the United States has always been a nation of immigrants, relatively few Americans speak a language other than English, and most of those who do are recent immigrants, along with their families. This US language paradox is compounded by the fact that, just as the world and the workplace have become so much more globalized and interconnected, fewer US students are studying foreign languages, especially at the college and university level.

Foreign language educators have long stressed the importance of foreign language skills and cultural knowledge and have advocated for foreign language learning. As early as 1940, in "A Factor in Presenting Our Product," Gilbert C. Kettelkamp wrote that "if teachers of foreign languages have faith in their product they should be willing to use all means available in presenting it to the public." In 1956, in *Language for Everybody*, Mario Pei wrote that knowledge of other languages "expands your horizon and makes accessible to you the treasuries of world thought." In 1961, in *Why Johnny Should Learn Foreign Languages?* Theodore Huebener wrote, "despite widespread popular interest in foreign languages, many educational administrators throughout the years have minimized their importance in our curriculum." In 2008, in *Educating Global Citizens in Colleges and Universities*, Peter Stearns wrote that America's "widespread hostility to seriously learning foreign languages has become almost legendary."

However, the most recent MLA Enrollment Survey, released in 2018, begins with "between fall 2013 and fall 2016, enrollments in languages other than English fell 9.2% in colleges and universities in the United States."

The disconnect between the acknowledged importance of foreign language skills and foreign language learning, and the numbers of students enrolled at the college and university level is evident. In fact, since the MLA began tracking enrollment in 1960, the percentage of college students enrolled in a course in a language other than English has decreased by more than half, from 16.2 percent in 1960 to 7.5 percent in 2016, the most recent year for which figures are available. A campaign for foreign languages is needed if we are to increase both awareness and motivation among students and their parents, as well as funding to expand access and opportunity and to support teacher training.

Foreign Language Advocacy
in the United States

The current conversation of foreign languages in the United States began with the 1979 report, *Strength through Wisdom: A Critique of U.S. Capability: A Report to the President from the President's Commission on Foreign Language and International Studies*, and the publication the following year of Senator Paul Simon's *The Tongue-Tied American: Confronting the Foreign Language Crisis*.

The United States government has supported the development of needed language skills through various initiatives, including The National Security Education Program, created by the 1991 National Security Education Act, and the critical languages initiative. Congressional hearings, including *The State of Foreign Language Capabilities in National Security and the Federal Government* (2000), *Closing the Foreign Language Gap: Improving the Federal Government's Foreign Language Capabilities* (2010), and *A National Security Crisis:*

Foreign Language Capabilities in the Federal Government (2012), have highlighted the lack of foreign language skills. In 2010, CIA Director Leon Panetta called for a national commitment to foreign language study, Secretary of Education Arne Duncan spoke of the need for increased funding for foreign language education, and Representative Rush Holt spoke of legislation he had introduced to increase Federal funding for foreign language education at the Foreign Language Summit in 2010. Numerous GAO reports, including *Foreign Language Capabilities: Departments of Homeland Security, Defense, and State Could Better Assess Their Foreign Language Needs and Capabilities and Address Shortfalls* (2010), have discussed the need for foreign language capabilities in the Federal Government.

Within the foreign language education professional community, the 2007 MLA report, *Foreign Languages and Higher Education: New Structures for a Changed World*, described the imperative for translingual and transcultural competence in a global world, and called for interdisciplinary and K-16 collaborations. After more than 10 years, the Languages for Specific Purposes (LSP) approach, including Business Language Studies (BLS), has offered an area of relative success, along with some pre-professional and area studies-type programs.

Other reports, most notably, *Securing America's Future: Global Education for a Global Age* (2003), *Education for Global Leadership: The Importance of International Studies and Foreign Language Education for U.S. Economic and National Security* (2006), *International Education and Foreign Languages: Keys to Securing America's Future* (2007), *What Business Wants: Language Needs in the 21st Century* (2009), and *Not Lost in Translation: The Growing Importance of Foreign Language Skills in the U.S. Job Market* (2017) describe and discuss the need for foreign language skills and the impact of the United States foreign language deficit on our economic and national security.

Foreign language educators have long been advocates for foreign language learning, and state, regional, and national professional associations, including the American Association of Teachers of

French (AATF), Central States Conference on the Teaching of Foreign Languages (CSCTFL), and the American Council on the Teaching of Foreign Languages (ACTFL), and many others, have advocacy groups. The Georgia Department of Education (GADOE) World Languages and Global/Workforce Initiative is an excellent example of state leadership in foreign language advocacy.

"Lead with Languages" is a national campaign launched in 2017 at the time of the publication of the AMACAD report, *America's Languages: Investing in Languages for the 21st Century*. Its goals are to increase enrollment, strengthen language programs, engage leaders, and build awareness. Another successful campaign is the Bilingual Revolution, with dual-language immersion programs in a dozen languages in public schools in New York City and elsewhere.

Beyond the United States, the European Union (EU) has promoted foreign language learning in alignment with its core value of multilingualism. In addition, the UK has promoted language learning through the *British Academy Languages Programme*, a collaboration on "The Case for Language Learning" series in the *Guardian*, the British Council report *Languages for the Future* (2013, 2017), *The CBI/Pearson Education and Skills Survey*, and new national foreign language curriculum (2016). In Ireland, a new 10-year plan to improve foreign language skills post-Brexit has been launched, building on a 2005 Forfas report, *Language and Enterprise: the Demand and Supply of Foreign Language Skills in the Enterprise Sector*. Australia has developed a second languages plan, the activity in the anglophone world confirming a global anglophone foreign language deficit. Many governments support language learning beyond their borders as part of their cultural diplomacy. The *Et en plus, je parle français* campaign launched by the Institut Français is an example.

The Many Languages One World Essay Contest and Global Youth Forum (MLOW), launched in 2013 by the United Nations Academic Impact, is intended to highlight the significance of multilingualism in the development of global citizenship and to encourage study of the six official languages of the UN.

Full-time college and university students can submit an essay on an assigned topic related to the role of multilingualism in global citizenship, in a learned second language that is also one of the official languages of the UN. Finalists are interviewed by Skype to confirm their language skills, and winners are brought, all expenses paid, to New York, where they have the opportunity to participate in a global youth forum on a local university campus where they interact as a global community as they work together in their language groups preparing their presentations on one of the principles of the UNAI (2014), or on one of the UN Sustainable Development Goals (SDGs) (2015-2017). The highlight of the week in the United States is the opportunity to present in the General Assembly Hall of the UN, always in the learned second language, the language of their winning essay.

The interactions among the student winners, representing countries from around the world, are interesting to observe, as they overcome linguistic and cultural barriers in order to communicate. The interactions are inspirational, however, in demonstrating the ability of people from diverse cultures to come together as one community, in both their day-to-day social interactions and as they come together in transnational teams to work together in a learned second language on their individual UN presentations within their language winner group.

The development of lasting friendships after only a brief, but intense, week together as a group is the most inspirational aspect of MLOW, confirmed by social media and email reports of local mini-reunions and encounters at international conferences. Many MLOW winners have also successfully gone on to advanced studies and to professional life, with multilingualism a valued part of their professional skills set. Within its UN context, MLOW is a high-profile example of multilingualism at work in developing and promoting the skills and values of global citizenship.

Overall, MLOW is a wonderful example of the many students from around the world who have developed impressive multilingual skills, in languages both closely related and apparently completely unrelated, to their mother tongue, through a variety of learning experiences. One characteristic shared by virtually all MLOW winners is a high level of motivation in language learning, demonstrated by their expertise in multiple languages, and a high degree of self-discipline, demonstrated by the fact that they even chose to enter the contest and compete, choosing to write a lengthy essay on a relatively abstract topic despite their typically busy schedules as university students.

Local applications of the MLOW experience may include, but are not limited to, student conferences and presentations on the Sustainable Development Goals, essay contests featuring essays in a learned second language, presentations by international students and students recently returned from study abroad on relevant topics, and the use of technology to offer students the opportunity to discuss global issues with students in another country or region.

A frustration expressed by many monolingual English-speaking American students is their inability to "make a difference," or to participate in the global conversation. MLOW certainly demonstrates the possibility of achieving multilingualism, with the motivation and effort. MLOW demonstrates that bridges to the future, bridges to success, and bridges among cultures are possible through multilingualism.

Multilingualism and Our Identity

In addition to being part of the global skills set, multilingualism is part of our personal and historical identity as Americans. Multilingual skills and cultural knowledge are certainly part of the global skills set. In learning another language, we develop the ability to better understand another culture, not only through its literature and media, but especially through conversation with others -- direct communication, without the barrier of a translation or interpretation. We are also better able to observe and come to understand how different cultures may approach a situation, a topic, or a task differently than we might, and to better understand another worldview.

Language is also part of who we are, of our personal and cultural identity, and the possibly of retaining a language spoken in the home or of re-learning a heritage language partially or completely lost in the American "melting pot" would not only benefit our society in terms of increasing our global skills and mindset, but also in terms of developing the sense of personal identity within each individual, and communication within our families and within our society.

As diversity, including linguistic and cultural diversity, has also been linked to creativity and effective problem-solving, encouragement of multilingualism is also encouragement of divergent thinking and carries with it the possibility of new approaches to solving long-standing problems and emerging local and global issues.

It is important to remember that millions of Americans speak a language other than English in the home, and that many more of us retain varying degrees of proficiency in family and heritage languages ranging from fluency to basic communicative skills, or just a few words. In addition, large areas of the United States have historically been home to a variety of European and other languages, with place names often the only sign of another linguistic community apparent to outsiders, and also home to local heritage language communities. In failing to promote multilingualism and foreign language learning, we deny ourselves the enjoyment, and the lessons of our history.

Soft power has been defined as "a persuasive approach to international relations, typically involving the use of economic or cultural influence" (*Oxford Dictionary*, n.d.). Language is certainly an element of soft power, which brings influence and opportunity to nations, organizations, and those who possess proficiency or fluency in said language. The global footprint of French and English, and international use of Spanish and Portuguese are a legacy of the colonial past, Russian is still frequently studied in areas of former Soviet influence, and Chinese is frequently studied throughout Asia. In 2017, France was the most visited country in the world, attracting nearly 90 million visitors, and ranked number one in terms of soft power (Gray, 2017).

The Framework of
Foreign Language Advocacy

Foreign language advocates can be found in business and industry, in government, and among foreign language educators. In order to be effective, foreign language advocacy needs to be evidence-based and data-driven, but most importantly, it needs to be proactive and personal, in close collaboration with communities and with foreign language stakeholders.

While the contemporary conversation on the foreign language deficit in the United States began with the publication of *The Tongue-Tied American* by Senator Paul Simon in 1980, current foreign language advocacy in the United States is framed by the following: *Foreign Languages and Higher Education: New Structures for a Changed World* (MLA, 2007) re-energized the conversation with its emphasis on translingual and transcultural competence as the goal and on the importance of both multiple pathways to the major and K-16 collaboration, making communication skills and cultural knowledge the goal of a potentially broad array of foreign language major pathways, and building on skills already acquired prior to college and university.

Other reports that form the foundation for current advocacy include, but are not limited to, the following (in reverse chronological order):

- *Enrollments in Languages Other Than English in United States Institutions of Higher Education* (2018)
- *The National K-12 Foreign Language Enrollment Survey Report* (2017)
- *America's Languages: Investing in Language Education for the 21st Century* (2017)
- *Not Lost in Translation: The Growing Importance of Foreign Language Skills in the U.S. Job Market* (2017)
- *A National Security Crisis: Foreign Language Capabilities in the Federal Government* (Senate Hearing, 2012)
- *Are Students Prepared for a Global Society?* (2011)
- *International Education and Foreign Languages: Keys to Securing America's Future* (2007)
- *Education for Global Leadership: The Importance of International Studies and Foreign Language Education for U.S. Economic and National Security* (2006)
- *Securing America's Future: Global Education for a Global Age* (2003)

Perspectives from beyond the United States include the following:

- *Languages for the Future* (2013,2017) -- UK
- *Key Data on Eurydice Report Teaching Languages at School in Europe* (2017) -- EC
- CBI/Pearson Education and Skills Survey 2017 -- UK
- *The Costs to the UK of Language Deficiencies as a Barrier to UK Engagement in Exporting* (2014) -- UK
- *Languages: The State of the Nation* (2013) -- UK
- *Study on the Contribution of Multilingualism to Creativity* (2009) -- EC
- *Languages and Enterprise The Demand & Supply of Foreign Language Skills in the Enterprise Sector* (2005) -- Ireland

The current conversation on foreign language advocacy began with the 1979 report, *Strength through Wisdom*, followed in 1980, by Senator Paul Simon's *The Tongue-Tied American*, as foreign language enrollments declined precipitously at the college and university level. The National Security Education and the Critical Languages scholarship program followed, while in the UK, the British Academy and the British Council launched language initiatives.

In the United States, the 2007 MLA report, *Foreign Languages and Higher Education: New Structures for a Changed World,* with its emphasis on translingual and transcultural competence, launched the next stage in the conversation on foreign languages, followed by *America's Languages* and the *National K-12 Foreign Language Enrollment Survey,* and the MLA enrollment survey in 2017 and 2018. Foreign language education professional associations have developed and implemented advocacy campaigns, but much more remains to be done.

Building the Foreign Language Skills We Need

In order to build the foreign language skills we need, a paradigm shift in attitudes toward foreign language learning is necessary, and foreign language advocacy is needed.

Motivation among greater numbers of students to begin foreign language study at a relatively early age, and to continue the study of one or more languages to proficiency, and even fluency, is needed. In order to create and sustain motivation, parental, school, and community support are necessary. In addition, the opportunity for continued foreign language study, with K-16 curricular pathways and collaborations, as well teacher training, need to be expanded. Heritage language and bilingual programs offer the best likelihood of achieving proficiency, and immersion is the methodology most likely to lead to successful learning outcomes.

In higher education, pre-professional foreign language programs, with opportunities for internships and experiential learning, and partnerships with language enterprise stakeholders to develop career pathways are needed.

To bring this about, foreign language advocacy -- specifically, a campaign for foreign languages, is needed. Foreign language educators, parents and community groups, and language enterprise stakeholders in business and government need to work together to bring about a resurgence of foreign languages. In addition, among foreign language educators, K-16 and interdisciplinary collaborations are essential.

Once a broad-based alliance of foreign language stakeholders has been established, the campaign needs to be strategic, framed by the psychology of influence, change management, beginning with "a sense of urgency" and social/cause marketing to promote language learning as a public good. In addition to its role in personal and professional success, multilingualism empowers those with foreign language skills and cultural knowledge to work together to effectively address complex social issues, both local and global.

Multilingualism
and the Sustainable Development Goals

Launched in 2013 as an initiative of the United Nations Academic Impact, the Many Languages One World Essay Contest and Global Youth Forum (MLOW), intended to highlight the role of multilingualism in global citizenship and to promote continued study of the official languages of the UN, invites college and university students from around the world to submit essays on an assigned topic related to the principles of the UNAI and, later, to the Sustainable Development Goals (SDGs) in a learned second language which is also one of the six UN official languages (Many Languages One World, n.d.).

The finalists are interviewed in the language of their essays, and the winners -- 10 for each of the six official languages -- are brought to New York where they have the opportunity to present, in the language of their essay, in the General Assembly Hall of the United Nations.

The camaraderie among students from around the world, demonstrated during their stay in New York, in social media, and in numerous local mini reunions, is remarkable and inspirational.

Chapter 9

Empowering Communities for a
Multilingual Future

___

W hile the idea of a global *lingua franca* has the strength of its simplicity, it is not without risk in terms of cultural loss among the languages that are not this *lingua franca*. In addition, the chosen language itself loses less frequently used elements as it spoken by more and more non-native speakers. There is also the moral dilemma of absolute power, in this case the power and influence of a global *lingua franca*, which "corrupts absolutely" (Acton Institute, n.d.). In addition, the goals of communicative and cultural competence transcend the myths (Grosjean, 2010) about multilingualism, which include the necessity of perfect and unaccented language, and offer a pragmatic path forward to multilingualism.

Decisions need to be made -- by educators, by business, by government, but especially by families, and by parents, working together collaboratively as partners --to ensure the best present and future for our children. It is no longer a question of anglophone Americans learning a "foreign" language sporadically in high school and/or college, it is more a question of reciprocal multilingualism, where we are all both mother tongue speaker and second language learner, in order to reduce social segmentation and to increase the overall social welfare (Caminal, 2016).

Bilingual and immersion education are among the most effective means to both address the United States foreign language deficit and to build the language skills needed in our multilingual communities. (Gross, 2016) confirms that there are over 2,000 dual language immersion programs in the United States.

Although dual-language education differs from traditional foreign/second language education in that it uses the language as a medium of instruction rather than viewing it as a subject (Garcia, 2009), foreign language stakeholders include parents and communities, business and government, and foreign language educators from both traditional and immersive learning environments.

In an examination of multilingualism and student achievement in dual-language (DL) programs, Lindholm-Leary (2016) found that both multilingualism and achievement benefit, with student progress toward multilingualism and achievement comparable to or higher than traditional English-language programs. However, continuation of dual-language instruction beyond the elementary grades remains both a challenge and goal.

An early start and continued progressive study are essential to develop effective foreign language skills. Elementary and even pre-K immersion programs are critically needed, as are opportunities for all interested learners to begin and pursue foreign language learning.

Fortune (2018) highlights the fact that the impact of multilingualism is not entirely quantitative, or skills-based, writing that "becoming bilingual leads to new ways of conceptualizing yourself and others. It expands your worldview, so that you not only know more, you know differently."

Paradoxically, just as globalization and an increasingly multilingual US make foreign languages an essential social, professional, and global skill, fewer US students are studying one or more languages to proficiency.

We need to embrace and advance homegrown multilingualism, but that can only happen if we offer these languages in public schools. Furthermore, immigrant children raised in environments that value the language of their parents learn the dominant language faster, as many of the studies show. Today, more and more students benefit from full-time dual-language programs in public schools and graduate fully bilingual, biliterate, and bicultural. However, the decision remains as to whether the personal, professional, and social benefits of foreign language skills and cultural knowledge outweigh the opportunity costs of acquiring foreign language skills instead of another skill.

Gregg Roberts once said that monolingualism is the illiteracy of the 21st century (Kluger, 2013). The personal, professional, and societal benefits of multilingualism and multiliteracy have been clearly demonstrated. The challenge remains as to how to build foreign language skills in the United States. Like many parents and educators, we are convinced that the cognitive, emotional, and social advantages of being multilingual and multiliterate are a universal gift that should be given to every child because it can constructively change our schools, our communities, and even our countries.

REFERENCES

Academy of Finland (2009). Brains benefit from multilingualism. *Science Daily* 26 Nov 2009. Web. Accessed 30 Nov 2018.

Adkins, S. (2016). *The 2015-2020 Digital Worldwide Digital English Language Learning Market.* Ambient Insight. Feb 2016. Web. Accessed 3 Dec 2018.

American Councils on International Education (2017). *The National K-12 foreign language enrollment survey.* Web. Accessed 30 Nov 2018.

Ayala, C. (2014). The Q & A: Rebecca Callahan. *Texas Tribune* 29 Oct 2014. Web. Accessed 30 Nov 2018.

BBC (2014). *Languages across Europe* (2014). Web. Accessed 30 Nov 2018.

Bel Habib, I. (2011). Multilingual skills provide export benefits and better access to new and   emerging markets. *Sens public: Revue web* 17 October 2011. Web. Accessed 30 Nov 2018.

Owler (n.d.) *Berlitz Competitors, Revenue, Number of Employees, Funding and Acquisitions.* Web. Accessed 30 Nov 2018.

Bhanoo, S. (2012). How Immersion Helps to Learn a New Language. *New York Times* 2 Apr 2012. Web. Accessed 30 Nov 2018.

Bialik, K. (2017). Number of U.S. workers employed by foreign-owned companies is on the rise. *Pew Research Center* 14 Nov 2017. Web. Accessed 30 Nov 2018.

Bialystok, E., Craik, F., I.M. & Luk, G. (2012). Multilingualism: Consequences for mind and brain. *Trends Cogn Sci.* 2012 Apr; 16(4): 240–250. PMC. Web. Accessed 30 Nov 2018.

Blatt, Ben (2014). Tagalog in California, Cherokee in Arkansas. What language does your state speak? *Slate* 13 May 2014. Web. Accessed 30 Nov 2018.

British Council (2013) *The English Effect.* Aug 2013. Web. Accessed 30 Nov 2018.

British Council (2013, 2017). *Languages for the future*. Nov 2013, Nov 2017. Web. Accessed 30 Nov 2018.

Byram, M. (2008). *From Foreign Language Education to Education for Intercultural   Citizenship: Essays and Reflections*. Bristol, UK: Multilingual Matters.

Callahan, R. M. & Gandara, P. C., eds. (2014). *The Bilingual Advantage: Language, literacy,   and the US labor market*. Bristol, UK: Multilingual Matters, 2014.

Canadian Heritage/Patrimoine canadien (2016). *Economic advantages of multilingualism: Literature review*. May 2016. Web. Accessed 30 Nov 2018.

CBI/Pearson Education and Skills Survey 2017. *Helping the UK thrive*. Web. Accessed 30 Nov 2018.

Center for Applied Linguistics. *Two-Way Immersion*. Web. Accessed 30 Nov 2018.

Chan, K. (2016). *These are the most powerful languages in the world*. 2 Dec. 2016. Web. Accessed 30 Nov 2018.

CIA News & Information (2010). *CIA Director Calls for a National Commitment to Language Proficiency at Foreign Language Summit*. 8 Dec 2010. Web. Accessed 30 Nov 2018.

CODOFIL. (n.d.). *French Immersion*. Web. Accessed 30 Nov 2018

Commission on Language Learning (2017). *America's languages: Investing in language education for the 21st century*. Web. Accessed 30 Nov 2018.

Committee for Economic Development (2006). *Education for Global Leadership: The   Importance of International Studies and Foreign Language*. Web. Accessed 30 Nov 2018.

Conner, C. (2014). How learning an additional language could influence your business. *Forbes* 17 Apr 2014. Web. Accessed 30 Nov 2018.

Cornick, M.F. & Roberts-Gassler, V. (1991). *The Value of foreign language skills for accounting and business majors. Journal of Education for Business* v. 86 n. 3, 161-163.

Couglan, S. (2017). Montreal ranked top city for students. *BBC News* 15 Feb 2017. Web. Accessed 30 Nov 2018.

Damari, R.R., et al. "The Demand for Multilingual Capital in the U.S. Labor Market." *Foreign   Language Annals*, 50(1), 13-37.

Di Paolo, A., and Tansel, A. (2015). *Returns to foreign language skills in a developing country: The Case of Turkey. Journal of Development Studies* v. 51 n. 4, 407-421.

CAL. (n.d.). *Directory of Foreign Language Immersion Programs in U.S. Schools.* Web. 30 Nov 2018.

Carnock J. and Garcia, A. *Dual Immersion Programs: How States Foster Expansion, Face Challenges.* New America. Blog. 21 Apr 2016. Web. Accessed 30 Nov 2018.

Georgia DOE. (n.d.). *Dual Language Immersion Programs in Georgia.* Web. Accessed 30 Nov 2018.

E-boost Consulting. (2013). *Five Minutes a Day: Six Sigma Marketing Strategy* (2013). 6 Dec 2013. Web. Accessed 30 Nov 2018

Economist Intelligence Unit (2012). *Competing across borders: How cultural and communication barriers affect business.* 25 Apr 2012. Web. Accessed 30 Nov 2018.

EF. 2018. *EF English Proficiency Index.* Web. Accessed 30 Nov 2018.

El Pais (2017). Number of Spanish speakers worldwide soars to 572 million. *El País.* 29 Nov 2017. Web. Accessed 3 Dec 2018.

Engel, J. S. (2014). *Global clusters of innovation: Entrepreneurial engines of economic growth around the world.* Cheltenham, UK: Elgar.

English, Chinese, and French most useful for business (2011). *Language Magazine.* Web. Accessed 30 Nov 2018.

Eurobarometer (2012). *Europeans and their languages, 2012.* 25 July 2012. Web. Accessed 30 Nov 2018.

Euronews (2018). *Poland's skilled workers attract global businesses.* 27 Feb 2018. Accessed 30 Nov 2018.

European Commission (2006). *Effects on the European economy of shortages of foreign language skills in enterprise.* Web. Accessed 30 Nov 2018.

European Commission (2009). *Study on the contribution of multilingualism to creativity.* Web. Accessed 30 Nov 2018.

European Commission (2012). Eurobarometer: 98% say language learning is good for their children, but tests highlight skills gap. 21 June 2012. Web. Accessed 30 Nov 2018.

European Parliament (2016). *Research for CULT committee -- European strategy for multilingualism: Benefits and costs.* 14 Oct 2016. Web. Accessed 30 Nov 2018.

Fairfax County Public Schools Immersion Programs. Web. Accessed 30

Nov 2018.

Fang, L. (2014). Where have all the lobbyists gone? *The Nation* 19 Feb 2014. Web. Accessed 30 Nov 2018.

FERDI (n.d.). *Francophonie would provide significant stability in times of crisis.* Web. Accessed 30 Nov 2018.

Forfás (2005). *Languages and enterprise: The Demand & supply of foreign Language skills in the enterprise sector.* 8 June 2005. Web. Accessed 30 Nov 2018.

Flaherty, C. (2018). L'Œuf ou la poule ? *InsideHigherEd* 19 Mar 2018. Web. Accessed 30 Nov 2018.

Florida, R. (2008). *Who's your city? How the creative economy Is making where to live the most important decision of your life.* NY: Basic, 2008.

Fortune, T. W. (n.d.). *What the research says about immersion.* Web. Accessed 30 Nov 2018.

French Morning (n.d.). *Bilingual fair.* Web. Accessed 30 Nov 2018.

Gala-Global (2018). *Translation and localization industry facts and data.* Web. Accessed 30 Nov 2018.

Garcia, O. ed. (2009). *Bilingual education in the 21st century: A Global perspective.* Chichester, UK: Wiley-Blackwell.

Gray, A. (2017). *France becomes the world No 1 for soft power.* 27 July 2017. Web. Accessed 30 Nov 2018.

Grosjean, F. (2010). *Bilingual: Life and reality.* Boston: Harvard University Press.

Gross, N. (2016). *The New Multilingualism.*

Grosse, C. U. (2004). *The Competitive advantage of foreign languages and cultural knowledge. The Modern Language Journal* v. 88 n. 3, 351-373.

Grosse, C. U., Tuman, W. V., and Critz, M.A. (1998). *The Economic utility of foreign   language study. The Modern Language Journal* v. 82 n. 4, 457-472.

Gunesch, K. (2008). *Multilingualism and cosmopolitanism: Meanings, relationships, tendencies.* Saarbrücken, Germany: Mueller.

Harris, E.A. (2015). Dual-language programs are on the rise even for native English   speakers. *New York Times* 8 Oct 2015. Web. Accessed 30 Nov 2018.

Hazlehurst, J. (2010). Learning a foreign language: Now you're talking. *Guardian* 27 Aug 2010. Web. Accessed 3 Dec 2018.

Hogan-Brun, G. (2017). *People who speak multiple languages make the best employees for one big reason.* 9 Mar 2017. Web. Accessed 30 Nov 2018.

Institute of International Education (2017). *Open doors report 2017.* Web. Accessed 30 Nov 2018.

National Research Council. (2007). *International Education and Foreign Languages: Keys to Securing America's Future* Web. Accessed 1 Dec 2018.

International Publishers Association. (2016). *Annual Report. 2015-2016.* Web. Accessed 1 Dec 2018.

International Trade Administration (2017). *Jobs supported by state exports.* Web. 1 Dec 2018.

Jaumont, Fabrice. The Bilingual Revolution: The Future of Education is in Two Languages. New York, NY: TBR Books, 2017.

Jaumont, F., Le Devedec, B. & Ross J. (2016). "Institutionalization of French Heritage Language Education in U.S. School Systems: The French Heritage Language Program" in

Kagan, O., Carreira, M., Chik, C. eds. *Handbook on Heritage Language Education: From Innovation to Program Building.* Oxford, U.K.: Routledge.

Jolin, L. (2014). Why language skills are great for business. *Guardian* 16 Dec 2014. Web. Accessed 1 Dec 2018.

Kharkhurin, A. V. (2012). *Multilingualism and creativity.* Bristol, UK: Multilingual Matters.

Kluger, J. (2013). The Power of the bilingual brain. *Time* 29 Jul 2013. Accessed 26 Jun 2018.

Kokemuller, N. (2018). What are the benefits of multilingualism in the workplace?

Kotter, J. *The 8-Step Process for Leading Change.* Web. Accessed 30 Nov 2018.

Language Immersion (9-12). *Houston Chronicle.* Web. Accessed 1 Dec 2018.

Language Flagship (2009). *What business wants: Language needs in the 21st century.* Web. Accessed 3 Dec 2018.

Lardinois, F. (2017). Duolingo raises 25M at a 700M valuation. *TechCrunch* 25 July 2017. Web. Accessed 30 Nov 2018.

Leach, N. (2016). Do you have a spare £66,000? Then learn Mandarin! Interactive map reveals the cost of mastering the world's top 20 languages. *Daily Mail* 3 Nov 2016. Web. 3 Dec 2018.

Learning English: Moving Words. *Nelson Mandela*. Web. Accessed 3 Dec 2018.

Lebov, Ray (2013). *Lobbying 101: What Makes an Effective Lobbyist.* Oct 2013. Web. Accessed 3 Dec 2018.

Lindholm-Leary, K. (2016). *Multilingualism and academic achievement in children in dual   language programs.* In Nicoladis, E., Montanari, S., eds. *Multilingualism across the lifespan: Factors moderating language proficiency.* Washington, DC: American Psychological Association.

Linguists Online: Language-Teaching Firms. (2013). *Economist* 5 Jan 2013. Web. Accessed 3 Dec 2018.

Livermore, D. (2016). *Driven by difference: How great companies fuel innovation through   diversity.* NY: AMACOM, 2016.

Lobbying (definition).   Web. Accessed 3 Dec 2018.

Lobbyit. (2016).   *Five Reasons to Lobby for your Cause.* 9 Oct. 2016. Web. Accessed 30 Nov 2018.

Lozano, R. (2018). *An American Language: The History of Spanish in the United States.* Oakland: University of California Press.

Lubin, G. (2017). Queens has more languages than anywhere in the world — here's where they're found. *Business Insider* 15 Feb 2017. Web. Accessed 3 Dec 2018.

Markarian, M. (2017) 11 Habits of highly effective lobbyists. *Huffington Post* 6 Dec 2017. Web. Accessed 30 Nov 2018.

McComb, C. (2001). *About One in Four Americans Can Hold a Conversation in a Second Language.* 6 Apr 2001. Web. Accessed 3 Dec 2018.

McNunn, R. (2017). 6 Top industries for multilingual employees. *Huffington Post* 27 Sept 2017. Web. Accessed 3 Dec 2018.

Meaghan (2018). *Sorry STEM, Google just made the case for more foreign language   education* 1 Jan 2018. Web. Accessed 3 Dec 2018.

Merritt, A. (2013). What motivates us to learn foreign languages? *Telegraph* 28 Feb 2013. Web. Accessed 3 Dec 2018.

Modern Language Association (2018). *Enrollments in languages other than English in United   States institutions of higher education.* Web. Accessed 3 Dec 2018.

Modern Language Association (2007). *Foreign Languages and Higher Education: New Structures for a Changed World.* Web. Accessed 3 Dec 2018.

Murray, J. (2014). Learning languages is key to UK's success in the global economy. *Guardian* 19 June 2014. Web. Accessed 3 Dec 2018.

NAFSA (n.d.). *NAFSA international student economic value tool.* Web. Accessed 3 Dec 2018.

The National Institute for Lobbying and Ethics (2017). Web. Accessed 3 Dec 2018.

Neeley, T., and Kaplan, R. S. (2014). What's your language strategy? *Harvard Business Review* Sept 2014. Web. Accessed 3 Dec 2018.

New American Economy (2017). *Not lost in translation: The Growing importance of foreign language skills in the U.S. job market.* Web. Accessed 3 Dec 2018.

Poppick, S. (2014). Want to boost your salary? Try learning German. *Time* 4 Jun 2014. Web Accessed 3 Dec 2018. Potowski, K. Handbook of Spanish as a heritage/minority language. (2017) (Edited) Routledge.

Potowski, K. Language diversity in the U.S.A. (Edited).(2010). Cambridge University Press.

Potowski, K. Rothman, J. Bilingual youth: Spanish-speakers in English-speaking countries. (2010). John Benjamins.

Potowski, K. Language and identity in a dual immersion school. (2007). Multilingual Matters.

Redden, Elizabeth (2017). Call to Action on Languages, 10 Years Later. *InsideHigherEd* 6 Jan 2017. Web Accessed 3 Dec 2018.

Report Buyer. *The Global online language learning market is forecasted to grow at CAGR of 1897 during the period 2017-2021.* (2017). 26 Dec 2017. Web. Accessed 30 Nov 2018.

Ross, J. (2019). Two Centuries of French Education in New York. New York, NY: TBR Books.

Ross, J.; Jaumont, F.; Schulz, J.; Ducrey, L.; Dunn, J. (2017) "Sustainability of French Heritage Language Education in the

United States" in Peter P. Trifonas and Thermistoklis Aravossitas (editors) International Handbook on Research and Practice in Heritage Language Education. New York, NY: Springer.

Ross, J. & Jaumont, F. (2014). "French Heritage Language Communities in the United States" in Terrence Wiley, Joy Peyton, Donna Christian, Sarah Catherine Moore, Na Liu. (editors). Handbook of Heritage and Community Languages in the United States: Research, Educational Practice, and Policy. Oxford, U.K.: Routledge

Ross, J. & Jaumont, F. (2012). Building Bilingual Communities: New York's French Bilingual Revolution" in Ofelia García, Zeena Zakharia, and Bahar Otcu, (editors). Bilingual Community Education and Multilingualism. Beyond Heritage Languages in a Global City (pp.232-246). Bristol, U.K.: Multilingual Matters.

Ross, J. & Jaumont, F. (2013). French Heritage Language Vitality in the United States." Heritage Language Journal. Volume 9. Number 3. Joint National Committee for Languages - National Council for Languages and International Studies.

Ryan, C. (2013). *Language Use in the United States: 2011.* US Census. Web. Accessed 3 Dec 2018.

Schroedler, T. (2018). The Value of foreign language learning: *A Study on linguistic capital   and the economic value of language skills.* Wiesbaden, Germany: Springer.

Seave, A. (2016). In the battle of online language learning programs, who is winning? *Forbes* 23 Sept 2016. Web. Accessed 3 Dec 2018.

Sercu, Lies (2006). "The Foreign Language and Intercultural Competence Teacher: the Acquisition of a New Professional Identity." *Intercultural Education,* 17 (1), 55-72.

Sitsanis, N. (2017) *Internet Users by Language: Top 10 Languages.* Web. Accessed 1 Dec 2018.

Statista. *Number of social media users worldwide from 2010 to 2021 (in billions).* Statista. Web. Accessed 3 Dec 2018.

Stearns, P. (2008). *Educating Global Citizens in Colleges and Universities: Challenges   and Opportunities.* New York:

Routledge.

Steele, J.L., et al. (2017). *Dual-language immersion programs raise student achievement in   English.* Rand Corporation. Web. Accessed 3 Dec 2018.

Stein-Smith, K.(2017). The Multilingual Advantage: Foreign Language as a Social Skill in a Globalized World. *International Journal of Humanities and Social Science* v. 7 no. 3 Mar 2017. Web. Accessed 3 Dec 2018.

Stein-Smith, K. (2013). *The US Foreign Language Deficit and Our Economic and National Security.* Lewiston, NY: Edwin Mellen Press.

Stein-Smith, K. (2013). *The US Foreign Language Deficit and How It Can Be Effectively Addressed in a Globalized World.* Lewiston, NY: Edwin Mellen Press.

Stein-Smith, K. (2016). *The US Foreign Language Deficit: Strategies for Maintaining   a Competitive Edge in a Globalized World.* NY: Palgrave Macmillan.

Stein-Smith, K. (2013). *The US Foreign Language Deficit.* TEDx. Web. Accessed 2 Dec 2018.

Tharoor, S. (2017). *There's One Country in the World where the Newspaper Industry Is Still Thriving.* World Economic Forum 24 May 2017. Web. Accessed 3 Dec 2018.

Trafton, A. (2018). Cognitive scientists define critical period for learning language. *MIT News* 1 May 2018. Web Accessed 3 Dec 2018.

Turner, C. (2015). *The 5 Traits of Winning Grassroots Campaigns.* 25 Feb 2015. Web. Accessed 30 Nov 2018.

UNESCO. *Diversity and the Film Industry.* Mar 2016. Info Paper 29. Web. Accessed 30 Nov 2018.

United Nations (2017). *SG on multilingualism -- a core value of the United Nations.* 19 July 2017. Web. Accessed 3 Dec 2018.

United States Census Bureau (2018) *Top trading partners.* Web. Accessed 3 Dec 2018.

United States Census Bureau (2011) *Overview of Race and Hispanic Origin: 2010.* Mar 2011. Web. Accessed 3 Dec 2018.

United States Department of Education (2017). *Teacher shortage areas nationwide listing 1990–1991 through 2017–2018.* Web. Accessed 3 Dec 2018.

United States Department of Labor. *Occupational Outlook Handbook. Translators and Interpreters.* Web. Accessed 3 Dec 2018.

Vanides, J. (2016). *4 Reasons why global fluency matters: an open letter to 6th graders   everywhere.* 9 Dec 2016. Web. Accessed 3 Dec 2018.

Villanova University. *Difference between: Six Sigma and Lean Six Sigma.* Web. Accessed 30 Nov 2018.

Villanova University. *Six Sigma: DMAIC Methodology.*   Web. Accessed 3 Dec 2018.

Young, H. The Digital Language Divide. *Guardian.* Web. Accessed 30 Nov 2018.

Thompson, A. (2016). How learning a new language improves tolerance. *The Conversation* 11 Dec 2016. Web. Accessed 3 Dec 2018.

Weinreich, U. (1968). *Languages in contact.* The Hague: Mouton.

Williams, D. R. (2011). Multiple language usage and earnings in Western Europe. *International Journal of Manpower.* v. 32 n. 4, 372-393.

INDEX

Index

135

About the Authors

Fabrice Jaumont is the author of *The Bilingual Revolution: The Future of Education is in Two Languages* (TBR Books, 2017), which provides inspirational vignettes and practical advice for parents and educators who want to create a dual-language program in their own school. He has also published several books and articles, including *Unequal Partners: American Foundations and Higher Education Development in Africa* (Palgrave-MacMillan, 2016); *Partenaires inégaux: fondations américaines et universités en Afrique* (Editions Maison des Sciences de l'Homme, 2018); *Stanley Kubrick: The Odysseys* (Books We Live by, 2018).

Fabrice Jaumont is a Research Fellow at Fondation Maison des Sciences de l'Homme in Paris. He is also Education Attaché for the Embassy of France to the United States, a Program Director for FACE Foundation in New York, and the founder of New York in French. Fabrice Jaumont holds a Ph.D. in Comparative and International Education from New York University. He was made a *Chevalier dans l'Ordre des Palmes académiques* by the Government of France and was awarded the *Prix de la diversité culturelle* by the *Organisation internationale de la Francophonie* and the Committee of French-speaking Ambassadors to the United Nations. For more information, visit the author's blog: fabricejaumont.net

Kathleen Stein-Smith is the author of *The U.S. Foreign Language Deficit: Strategies for Maintaining a Competitive Edge in a Globalized World* (Palgrave-MacMillan, 2016), *The U.S. Foreign Language Deficit and How It Can Be Effectively Addressed in the Globalized World: A Bibliographic Essay* (Edwin Mellen Press, 2013), and *The U.S. Foreign Language Deficit and Our Economic and National Security: A Bibliographic Essay on the U.S. Language Paradox.* (Edwin Mellen Press, 2013).

Kathleen Stein-Smith is Associate University Librarian and Adjunct Faculty in Foreign Languages at Fairleigh Dickinson University; Chair of the American Association of Teachers of French Commission on Advocacy; a member of the American Translators Association Education & Pedagogy Committee; and an advisor to the Central States Conference on the Teaching of Foreign Languages, the Northeast Conference on the Teaching of Foreign Languages), and Southern Conference on Language Teaching. She also serves as French Language Facilitator at Many Languages One World. She has delivered a TEDx talk, *The U.S. Foreign Language Deficit—" What It Is; Why It Matters; and What We Can Do about It"*, and maintains a blog, "Language Matters." She holds a Ph.D. in Interdisciplinary Studies from Union Institute & University, and was made a *Chevalier dans l'Ordre des Palmes académiques* by the Government of France.

About TBR Books

TBR Books is a program of the Center for the Advancement of Languages, Education, and Communities. We publish researchers and practitioners who seek to engage diverse communities on topics related to education, languages, cultural history, and social initiatives. We translate our books in a variety of languages to further expand our impact. Become a member of TBR Books and receive complimentary access to all our books.

- Fabrice Jaumont and Kathleen Stein-Smith's *The Gift of Languages: Towards a Paradigm Shift in Foreign Language Education* is available on our website and on all major online bookstores as a paperback and e-book.
- Fabrice Jaumont's *The Bilingual Revolution: The Future of Education is in Two Languages* is available on our website in Arabic, English, French, German, Russian, Spanish, and soon in Chinese, Italian, Japanese, and Polish.

For a listing of all books published by TBR Books, information on our series, or for our submission guidelines for authors, visit our website at

http://www.tbr-books.org

About CALEC

The Center for the Advancement of Languages, Education, and Communities is a nonprofit organization with a focus on multilingualism, cross-cultural understanding, and the dissemination of ideas. Our mission is to transform lives by helping linguistic communities create innovative programs, and by supporting parents and educators through research, publications, mentoring, and connections.

We have served multiple communities through our flagship programs which include:

- TBR Books, our publishing arm; which publishes research, essays, and case studies with a focus on innovative ideas for education, languages, and cultural development;

- TheBilingualRevolution.info, an online platform which provides information, coaching, support to multilingual families seeking to create dual-language programs in schools;
- NewYorkinFrench.net, an online platform which provides collaborative tools to support New York's Francophone community and the diversity of people who speak French.

We also support parents and educators interested in advancing languages, education, and communities. We participate in events and conferences that promote multilingualism and cultural development. We provide consulting for school leaders and educators who implement multilingual programs in their school. For more information and ways you can support our mission, visit

http://www.calec.org